BURGLAR-PROOFING YOUR HOME

RALPH TREVES

THEODORE AUDEL & CO.

a division of

HOWARD W. SAMS & CO., INC.

4300 West 62nd Street
Indianapolis, Indiana 46268

ISBN: 0-672-23809-8

Manufactured in the United States of America

Contents

1

How Safe
is Your Home?

It is frightening and heartbreaking to return home one evening to find that someone has broken in, ransacked the closets, upturned all the dresser drawers, and made off with your silverware and clothing, your coin collection, and your wife's jewels.

This, unfortunately, is not an unusual occurrence. Each year, more than a million American homes (yes, a *million!*) are broken into and looted. More than half of these burglaries took place during the daytime. The number of burglaries has more than doubled in the past decade, resulting in annual losses of an estimated billion dollars in stolen articles and property damage. And no cost can be set on serious injuries to residents from physical encounters with the prowlers.

While the city apartment dweller still is the most frequent victim of housebreaking, the crime wave has spread rapidly into the formerly safe and placid suburbs, small towns, and even rural areas. Every section of the country is affected. There just aren't any "good" neighborhoods any more!

Even the home of a police chief is not immune. In San Jose, California, thieves pried open a window of Chief Blackmore's home, ransacked all the rooms, and made off with his stereo system, television set, and some cash. It was the fourth house on the chief's block to be broken into in less than two months.

Financially damaging as burglaries may be, a more serious consequence is the persistent fear, often of panic proportions, that now obsesses so many families, so that even your children, just as your wife and yourself, are unable to sleep peacefully, constantly alert for strange sounds in the night, expecting to be pounced upon at any moment by an intruder. Others, particularly single people living alone, are afraid to come home in the evening, for fear of encountering a burglar inside.

You're on Your Own. If nothing like this has happened, you've been exceedingly lucky, or have taken adequate protective measures. Many families not so fortunate have been aroused to the need for better home security only after sad experience. But for those who have so far escaped this trouble, it's foolhardy to continue relying on common locks, archaic window latches, and limited police protection. Police patrols are indeed an essential line of defense, and they keep up an unrelenting drive on prowlers. The F.B.I. has stated, however, in its annual U.S. *Crime Reports,* that law enforcement agencies no longer can cope adequately with this crime of stealth, and in fact have been able in recent years to apprehend only about 20 per cent of the offenders.

A Change for the Worse. Not many years ago families could feel quite safe and relaxed in their homes without making a big thing about security measures. Only the most simple protective routine was relied upon, and sometimes none at all, with rarely any dire consequences. Nighttime lockup was perfunctory—usually just slipping the door bolt or turning the key. Homeowners seldom bothered to close their downstairs windows, especially if there were screens, which were considered a sufficient barrier. Doors were left open all day, and often in the evening too. When the family went out, the door key more often than not was handily slipped under the mat or over the door frame.

Locks in many cases were of easily jimmied spring-latch design. While the front door might have a secure cylinder lock, the fact that the bolt had to be turned separately with the key to lock it from the outside, meant that it was mostly neglected as too inconvenient. The rear kitchen and porch doors were usually fitted with the kind of mortise lock that is opened with a "skeleton" key.

Cellar doors more often than not were held with just a barrel bolt or hook-and-eye fastener. And even this kind of rudimentary security was not always utilized – if someone in the family remembered at the movies that he or she had forgotten to lock the door, that was no cause for worry.

Things are Different Now. You don't have to study the crime statistics to realize the extent of the burglary menace now. However, knowing the facts should not only encourage you to act for your own protection, it should provide clues to the direction that your defense efforts must take to assure effective results.

Burglary is defined in different ways in different states, but it is defined by the Crime Statistics Bureau as unlawful entry, or attempt at such entry, to commit a felony or theft, even though no force is used to gain entrance.

A total of 2,169,300 burglaries were reported in the F.B.I. *Unified Crime Reports* for the year 1970, of which 58 per cent or more than 1,200,000 were residence burglaries. The incidence of burglaries rose by 142 per cent from 1960 to 1970, including an 11 per cent rise from 1969 to 1970.

Not All Thefts Reported. Startling as it is, this figure of 1,200,000 home burglaries may be far too conservative. The President's Commission on Law Enforcement and Administration has said that property crimes were more than triple the rate indicated by the F.B.I. reports. The Commission report, titled *The Challenge of Crime in a Free Society,* cited detailed surveys in several major cities which showed that the burglary rate for individual victims was more than 300 per cent greater than that reported by the F.B.I.

The chief explanation for this disparity was that many victims failed to report burglary losses because they felt that the police "could not do anything" to halt the thefts or to recover the stolen articles. Some of the reluctance to report burglaries probably was due to fear that insurance companies would cancel their policies, which in a sense tends to inflict added punishment on the helpless victim rather than on the perpetrator of the crime.

There is another statistical factor of importance: when an unlawful entry includes a violent attack upon an occupant, the offense is listed as a robbery rather than a burglary. Such encounters with a desperate, cornered prowler often result in serious injuries to the resident. Fortunately, such incidents are comparatively infrequent, with less than 32,000 attacks on residents occurring during the more than a million home burglaries. This figure covers only cities encompassing less than half the total national population; data on rural and small town incidents, which are not available, might well double it.

Daytime Burglaries Soaring. Over the period from 1960 to 1970, daytime burglaries of residences increased by an astounding and ominous 337 per cent. The rise in the last year alone of that period was 13 per cent, an increase far greater than that for nighttime thefts. The obvious inferences to be drawn are that homeowners have not yet applied adequate security routines to the family daytime practices, and that the type of criminal involved is steadily changing from that of a nighttime prowler to a younger, opportunity-seeking element that can operate more openly without attracting suspicious attention.

This latter group apparently consists mainly of teenagers and youths, and even young girls, who may be taken as friends of neighbors, or as legitimate delivery or service personnel. In any event, the young person is less likely to be challenged as he walks to the side door of a home, or loiters in an apartment corridor. And it takes him (or her) just a moment to enter if the door is held with a flimsy lock that just needs a push to crash it open, or a plastic window screen that can be sliced apart with a razor blade.

Perhaps a contributing element is that more women are joining the labor force, leaving the home or apartment unattended and easy prey during the daytime hours, a time when the noise of breaking window glass or splintering doors will less likely be noticed. Also, there is the understandable tendency to relax security during the day, allowing doors to remain unlocked, windows open, and alarm turned off, even when no one is at home.

The marauders seem to have caught onto this. Instead of prowling under cover of darkness at night, they are finding it safer and easier to operate under the cover of daytime noise, the diverted attention of neighbors, and relaxed security measures.

A Year 'round Crime. Burglars know no season. The peak month in 1967 was December, but in the following year the peak month switched to July, and in 1970 was back to December. Draw whatever conclusions you may from that!

Every Section Affected. No part of the country is spared the soaring burglary incidence. In 1969, California had the highest burglary rate, with 1,676 incidents per 100,000 population, Florida was second with 1,358, and third place was tied by both Hawaii and New York with 1,304 each. The Southern states had 27 per cent of the total burglary volume, and in 1970 experienced the sharpest increase, 14 per cent, in the burglary rate.

Suburbs, Small Towns Feel Rise. In every type of community, and every stratum of society, homes are no longer safe from intrusion. Big cities, those over 250,000 population, have always borne the brunt of this crime, both in number of incidents and rate proportionate to the population. The rural areas fare best, with an average of 434 per 100,000 population, compared to 872 for suburban centers, and 1,948 for metropolitan cities. In the most recent report, however, suburban and rural areas suffered the largest rate of increase, each up 12 per cent.

In the cities, housebreaking isn't limited to the congested tenement districts, New York City's Park Avenue apartments and expensive hotels are constant victims despite their extensive protective arrangements of doormen, elevator operators, maids and butlers. Recent incidents were the robberies of Sophia Loren and Zsa Zsa Gabor in famous Park Avenue hotels. One result has been the widespread installations of burglar alarms in the more affluent private home sections. Now the alarm bell boxes high on outside walls are almost as common as television aerials.

In California's movieland, the palatial homes of famed film personalities in Beverly Hills, Bel Air, Newport, and Brentwood, are broken into time and again. Recent targets were the homes of John Wayne, Gregory Peck and Joe E. Brown. One of the 1970 Hollywood burglaries resulted in the loss of a Raphael painting, "The Peruzzi Madonna," valued at $1.2 million dollars. The burglary occurred while the owner was away from home for just one hour. Quite a number of lesser starlets, living in modest Hollywood apartments, have found on returning from work that their belongings had been ransacked by an intruder. Their greatest fear is that of coming home while the burglar is still in the apartment, or awakening at night and surprising a dope-crazed prowler.

Crash Any Barrier? You often hear the remark that "There's no way to stop a burglar—if he wants to get in, he can always do it." This defeatist notion is not justified. Instead, a determined and intelligent effort usually can overcome the menace, because every householder has definite advantages on his side.

A burglar will tackle any obstacle if he believes there's plenty of loot to be had. So your first objective is to avoid letting information get around, in the neighborhood and elsewhere, about any large sums of money, valuable jewelry, or other marketable possessions. In fact, you should make every effort to avoid attracting interest in your home for a "caper," as the street denizens say.

And while thieves are capable of breaking through almost any barriers when they are determined to do so, it is also a fact that they tend to pick the easiest and least risky targets. So your second objective is to make your home as impregnable as you can, so that entry would be obviously difficult, noisy, and dangerous.

The practical defense measures you must take vary according to the particular circumstances in your home. Knowing the nature of the burglar provides a measure of his capabilities and methods to be counteracted. The house burglar of today is nearly always a delinquent teenager or drifting youth, poorly equipped, relying mainly on stealth and opportunity. But never forget that he doesn't hesitate to splinter a door or break a window glass to get inside.

This is not to imply that all burglaries are casual and easygoing, aimed at a quick grab for whatever loot can be obtained. On the contrary, many seem to be planned with accurate knowledge about a large sum of money or particular jewelry in the house, and in those cases entry is forced by ruthlessly demolishing protective barriers, or by cunningly bypassing alarm systems. Homes and offices of doctors are frequent targets, possibly because they are expected to yield narcotics as well as usual valuables. In some homes, fully protected with excellent door locks, window gratings, and extensive alarm systems, thieves break in by cutting through the roof, or penetrating a wall from an adjacent garage. On occasion, residents are brutally pistol-whipped and tortured to open a safe or reveal the hiding place of their valuables.

Other Home Hazards. Concern with the growing crime threat should not divert attention from the ever-present menace of fire and other perils which exist within the home itself. Also, the present high cost of maintenance and repair services often leads to neglect or delay of essential upkeep, inevitably resulting in rapid deterioration of valuable property and the development of dangerous conditions.

One example of such combined damage and danger is a clogged roof gutter, which causes an ice dam in winter. Since the thawed water can't run off, it seeps into the eaves and dampens the walls and ceiling. Plaster, when wet, loses its bond to the lathing, and the ceiling ultimately may come down without warning in massive, heavy chunks, periling

any person in the room. Roof gutters need regular seasonal
cleaning. After correction of any roof leak, the firmness of
nearby ceiling areas should be tested and any loose sections
knocked down. In doubtful situations, the entire ceiling usually must be done over.

Fire Warning System. The most feared home hazard is
that of fire, and with justification. Fires and explosions
destroy or damage more than 600,000 one-and-two family
homes and other dwelling units, and take about 6,000 lives
annually in the U.S. A careful program of prevention, based
on familiarity with the causes of fire, explosions, and burns,
together with a dependable fire warning system, will ease
your mind and protect your family and home.

Other causes of serious injury in the home are falls due to
shaky stair railings and encumbrances, structural defects,
electrical shock, cuts, accidental poisoning, falling objects,
and those resulting from careless or improper use of tools,
appliances, and firearms. Knowledge of these dangers and
alertness in spotting such hazards to persons and threats to
the property itself, will help to eliminate them.

"Acts of God." When the disaster of a hurricane, earth
tremor, forest fire, mudslide or tidal flood strikes, there's
nothing much that can be done that had not already been
done. Earthquakes can happen anywhere, but some sections
are more susceptible than others. Cyclones and other major
storms are even less predictable. The homeowner can profit
from expert opinion, however, planning ahead to reduce such
destruction as was caused by the mudslides that occurred in
1969 on the Pacific Palisades, the 1970 forest fires, or some of
the Gulf Coast hurricanes.

Nearly all homes now are protected from lightning bolts
by their grounded electrical system. In some situations, however, subsequent construction work may affect the original
grounding effectiveness of the system, and a periodic checkup
is advised.

Environmental Invasions. Another condition only recently receiving the attention it deserves is the invasion of residential areas by industries, institutional facilities, and even municipal plants that pollute the area with obnoxious odors, cause excessive noise and traffic even at night, accumulate huge piles of trash, or blanket the neighborhood with smoke, dust, or radioactivity. Homeowners and residents need not yield to this imposition in subdued resignation.

There are several ways to ward off a threatening or even existing condition, ways that have in many cases been successful in protecting the neighborhood. Similarly, property damage to individual homes, such as cracked foundation walls done by blasting for nearby construction, may be recoverable by proper measures.

How Much Protection? Attitude is a vital factor in shaping your defenses. You should recognize that there is no such thing as absolute and total safety—the only place that comes near that concept is a prison cell with constant guards. So whatever provisions you make for your personal and home protection, there must necessarily be a compromise between total security and the requirements of normal daily living. Any program that fails to meet this standard indicates a surrender to fear.

You wouldn't want to live behind barred windows just to avoid a possible intrusion. Nor would you choose a watchdog to protect you that is so wild and ferocious that it might maim or kill an innocent neighbor—or even turn against you at some provocation.

The important thing is to strike a balance, accurately defining the menace, and proportioning the measures necessary to defeat it. The weight of this presentation is that most burglaries and home accidents are made possible by carelessness and neglect; and that careful adherence to the *Habit of Safety* can give you the best chance to avoid being victimized by the wave of crime.

Large companies and industrial plants employ security

consultants to plan controls against thefts, intrusions, and other crimes. Such professional services are not usually available to individuals. This book is intended to fill the gap so that the sanctity, the privacy, and the safety of the home can be maintained. Readers often can obtain advice on specific problems from some of the companies producing or selling burglary protection materials, but it is necessary to caution you against self-serving recommendations.

2

No Admittance!

The elements of a home defense program may be classified as follows:

1. Avoid attracting the attention of housebreakers.
2. Provide adequate barriers to entry.
3. Keep an alarm system or a watchdog on the alert.
4. Set up a security room for family retreat.

These four elements for burglary protection all depend on one underlying factor: the Habit of Safety, which is the human factor that forms the cornerstone of your efforts, and on which success depends.

Prowlers Keep Out! The first objective of your program is to avoid attracting the attention of a potential burglar to you or to your home. Whatever the extent of your affluence, there's no glory in flashing your diamonds while shopping for the family groceries, or pulling out a big wad of bills to pay a car repair bill. Instead, pay by credit card or charge account whenever possible. At your home, let delivery-men wait at the door, or allow them only into the kitchen if necessary, so that as few people as possible get a view of the house layout, particularly the location of the burglar-alarm control box. You might be confident that your local trades-people do not have dishonest employees, but youngsters have a tendency to describe an impressive home setting to friends or schoolmates whom you do not know.

Even for obviously prosperous homes, it's a good policy to keep the family Cadillac or Continental, and that sporty runabout, out of sight and in the garage. Luxurious lawn settings and swimming pools might well be screened by a high board fence or shrubs; they won't keep a burglar out, but they're less likely to invite him in.

There's no need to disguise or hide your protective measures, however. Evidences of well-planned security such as an alarm box high on the wall, a red alarm indicator light, steel gratings over basement window wells, and well-polished solid-looking door locks may effectively discourage a prospective intruder.

Thieves go primarily for money. They'll look for jewelry and other articles, but usually only if not enough cash has been found. They know that their risk is greatly multiplied if they are caught with "the goods," and at best they'll have to dispose of the stolen articles for very little money, regardless of their value.

A good rule for the homemaker is never to accumulate large sums of cash at home. That's what banks are for. It's safer and more efficient to keep on hand only such amounts as are needed for everyday purposes. Elimination or reduction of cash hoards, if that were generally adopted, could well bring a downturn in the number of burglaries.

But don't go to the other extreme and strip your house of all cash. There's an old folk lore, tried and proven for many decades and still valid, that it's wise to leave something for the crook. Empty-handed burglars can become so mean and frustrated that they go on a rampage of malicious destruction, slashing upholstered furniture, ripping clothing, smashing chairs, even deliberately blocking the sink drains while the water is turned on full force. The simple solution often is effective: keep $10 or $20 in an obvious place where it will

The sensible precautions pointed up in the sketch can become part of the family's routine. Check them off for your home by the numbers on the sketch. 1. Keep garage door always closed, with a lock as secure as the one on the front door. 2. Make sure front and back doors have night deadbolts in addition to spring latches. 3. Outside lights are a strong deterrent to burglars; there should be one covering every point of entry. 4. Don't keep large amounts of cash or valuable jewelry in the house. 5. Basement entry should preferably be covered with steel doors; padlock hasp should have all screws covered when locked. 6. Shades should be left at usual level when family is away, not tightly drawn. 7. Basement windows are covered with heavy wire mesh. 8. Plantings are trimmed so they won't screen a burglar's entry. 9. Don't hide the door key under the doormat, or on the door frame or in the mailbox. 10. Stop deliveries when the family is away. 11. A ladder is best locked with a chain or stored in a locked place.

be found. Loss of a small sum is insignificant if it prevents such vicious and costly vandalism.

No Easy Pickings. Home safety is not to be had just by wishing or hoping. It takes time and effort for planning the protective program, complete cooperation from all members of the family in carrying out the necessary routine, and also the expenditure of a modest amount for whatever hardware is required to do the job. Pennypinching thrift that postpones action often has a disastrous sequel.

Making a Security Survey. A first step in the security program is to make a careful and complete inspection of your home premises to spot vulnerable points of entry, judging them always from the point of view of the possible prowler. Carry along a small note book to jot down your findings for correction. Are there clumps of bushes around the side or rear door that would provide convenient cover while a thief is forcing the door or breaking a window? Perhaps trimming the bushes lower or aiming a flood light at that location will correct the situation. Does a large tree limb extend close to an upper porch deck or open window? Pruning the tree will eliminate the problem. Is the side door of the garage left unlocked, enabling an intruder to hide there while watching the movements of the household? Are your telephone wires exposed so they can be clipped easily, cutting you off from help? The wires can be protected with conduit, or shifted to rooftop level. Does your dog bark habitually at night, canceling his value as a watchdog? Does every exterior door with glass panels have a double-cylinder lock which requires a key to open it from the inside, and is that key kept at an inaccessible distance from the door? Are all ladders on the premises secured with padlocks or otherwise out of reach? If you have sliding glass patio doors, do they have a Charley-bar or extra throw bolt, as illustrated, so the door can't be lifted off the track? Are basement windows and similar means of entry protected with metal guards or areaway gratings? Are your special valuables kept in a vault or well protected closets, and do you keep a list of their identifying serial numbers?

To SUM UP: a home is relatively safe if all doors have solidly mounted dead-bolt locks, the windows are all closed and latched at night, the rear yard adequately lighted, basement windows and glass panel doors protected with metal guards, all keys strictly controlled and accounted for, callers always identified through the viewer before you open the door, and there is an effective burglar alarm system that is kept on alert, or a dependable watchdog. This routine is not particularly difficult, and soon becomes established as a habit of safety. But a single door or window left unlatched, or the one time

Sliding patio doors must have an adequate locking device. A horizontal "Charlie" bar across the closed door prevents easing the door out of its tracks.

the alarm is not set, cancels all your efforts and is an invitation to burglary.

Selective Purchases. Spurred by incidents of housebreaking in the neighborhood, homeowners rush out to the hardware store for additional locks and door chains, buying whatever types are available. Often these purchases are influenced by extravagant claims for "pickproof" locks.

Responsible dealers usually will remind you that even a very good lock is no better than the door on which it is installed. Burglars rarely bother to pick a lock unless it's an easy type with a well-worn keyway. Most often, a door is forced by the leverage of a jimmy or heavy screwdriver inserted between the door and jamb. A lock, any lock, won't defeat a really determined burglar, but a good dead-bolt lock in a solid door jamb can make breaking in so slow and noisy that the thief may give it up as a bad job.

Door chains are fine, ever so good-looking in polished brass and trim lines. But these are sold with tiny screws that won't offer much resistance to a determined thrust. Not only are longer screws advisable, the chain should be mounted in such a way as to provide minimum leeway or leverage to an attacker. Enough opening to identify a caller, or receive a letter, is sufficient.

3

Watching Your Step: The Habit of Safety

Whatever security devices and barriers you have installed, everything still will depend on how fully the Habit of Safety becomes part of the pattern of living for every member of your family. Even the finest lock won't do much good if the spare key is hanging on a nail in plain sight of a prowler in the garage, or a duplicate has been made by some part-time helper in the car wash where you left all the house keys in the ignition lock. What kind of security does a kitchen screen door provide if all the family is watching television in the den?

Home security takes a price, not so much in money, but rather of constant alertness and adherence to specific safety rules, even if they require some daily inconveniences and changes in long-established routines.

Who's There? Everyone knows how important it is not to open the door until the caller is positively identified, through the viewer or intercom, as *someone who is known and trusted*. Yet time after time, serious incidents occur because of carelessness about this fundamental rule. That certainly makes it easy for criminals: why take all the risk and bother about breaking in when people accommodatingly open the door.

A set of rules should be established at your home, to be followed by every member of the family. Use the viewer to scan the stoop or hallway, and refuse to open unless the caller is known. If the door must be opened, first put on the chain so that your observation can be confirmed. These steps are necessary and justified, so don't feel that you will be considered fussy or overcautious.

Make sure the outside light is bright enough so that you can observe the caller. This may be a problem in some apartment corridors where lighting is provided at minimum level. Local ordinances in some cities now require adequate illumination in apartment house hallways and lobbies, in addition to spotlights at service entrances. Even so, vandals have made a practice before invading apartments of breaking the lamps to assist their getaway and hinder identification. Your suspicion should be aroused whenever the lights are found to be sabotaged. Notify the "super" by telephone, and try to remain inside the apartment for the evening, or until the condition is corrected.

If your door viewer doesn't cover enough of the outside area, so that someone standing at the side can't be seen, get the improved swivel-type viewer that permits sighting side to side, and even downward.

You even have to be watchful when entering your home that there is no one loitering or hiding nearby who will simply slip inside just as you unlock the door, holding a sharp knife against your body to keep you silent. And silent you should be under the circumstances—just hand over your cash and hope the intruder leaves.

Phony "Home Buyers." With the more frequent daytime burglaries, a favorite recent trick for gaining admittance is worked by a man-woman team posing as possible home buyers. A For Sale sign is like an engraved invitation. The pair can roam the house, spotting the possible locations of money or jewelry, making sure no one else is at home, and sometimes even taking the precaution of clipping the telephone wires

Eye-level lens gives wide-angle view of entrance area. The rotating viewer shown covers greater area than stationary type.

or burglar alarm system. Then, they make quick work of grabbing whatever they can and make a getaway in a car parked around the corner. Listing a home for sale through a legitimate local realtor can help avoid such dangerous invasions.

Another gimmick is to lift a woman's pocketbook in a department store, then telephone to tell the victim that her bag had been found intact and that she should return to the store to claim it. As soon as she leaves the house, the thieves are waiting to enter with the keys found in the bag.

The decline of Western Union may be a blessing in at least one way, the virtual disappearance of the messenger boys and with them that old "telegram delivery" trick of gaining admittance. But in its place has come the "package for you" or even that real oldie, "flower delivery" that few seem able to resist. If you insist on opening up in these instances, keep the chain on while you obtain and sign (and inspect) any necessary receipt, then instruct the deliveryman to leave the package outside the door as you "can't take it in just now."

Installation of Peek-O-Viewer requires drilling a hole through the door. Locate a position that will be clear of any obstruction, mark center with awl.

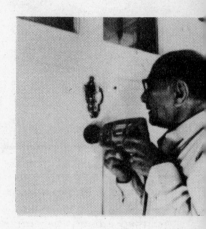

A hole saw will drill the required 2 ⅜-inch hole. If necessary use a 2 ¼-inch hole cutter and enlarge the hole with a rasp. Start the pilot drill in the marked hole, hold the drill straight in and drill to full depth of the hole-saw cup, which will be about half the thickness of the door.

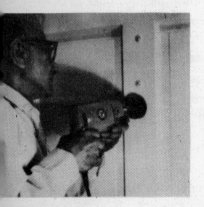

The pilot bit penetrates the entire door thickness, thus providing the guide for starting the drilling with the hole saw from the inside surface.

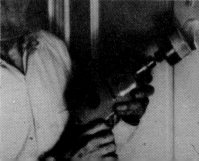

Cutting completed, core is removed intact with the hole saw.

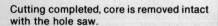

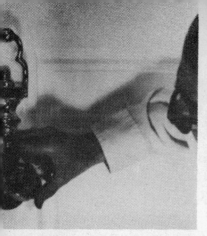

Rotating viewer section is inserted through exterior door surface. Plate on interior side locks the assembly securely together, and the installation is completed.

More Daytime Tricks. Perhaps these daytime hoodlums are getting more shrewd, as demonstrated by this incident: A young man rings the door bell and announces that he had "just damaged your car outside" and wants to leave his name so you can send him the repair bill. This happened at a home of a very quiet and careful family. When that reasonable statement opened the door, a couple of thugs rushed in, accompanied their demands for "your diamonds" by seriously injuring one of the family. In this case, the door viewer was used, but the second man had remained pressed against the side wall, out of the viewer's visibility range. Had the door been kept on the chain, even though opened, entry would have been prevented. As it was, some $20,000 in diamond rings and cash was taken.

Your Defense Plans are Secret. While there's no purpose in covering up the fact that your home is well protected, at the same time you must keep the inside arrangements as "classified secrets." The fewer people the better, who know the location of your alarm cutoff switch, what types of detectors are used, whether you have an open or closed circuit alarm (very important information for skilled burglars) and other details. Particularly with delivery boys and servicemen—the right thing is not to leave them unattended anywhere in the house. For example, snipping the open-circuit

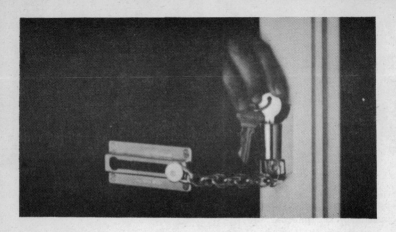

Chain with lock can be attached from outside when leaving the apartment.

wire takes just a second and negates your entire alarm system. A duplicate key or bending of a detector contact of a door alarm means open sesame to an intruder.

Hold on to Your Keys. There is much misunderstanding of the ways in which keys can be duplicated. It is not necessary for the person to have the key long enough to get the duplicate made with a keymaking machine. All he needs is an impression of the key in candle wax, plaster, or other suitable medium—then the copy can be produced from the correct key blank by filing the notches indicated by the depression. Duplicates can be made also from the numbers stamped on the key.

Changing Lock Cylinder. Any suspicion that a key is lost or missing, or may have gotten into wrong hands, should prompt immediate change of the lock cylinder. This is a simple matter, particularly if you keep extra cylinders with their keys on hand. Perhaps the cylinder you take out now can be put back again at some future date when another change is indicated, so save it with its set of keys. A more thorough measure would be to have the cylinder code changed each time, with new keys made, as described in the lock section.

One extra detail: keep a record of the serial numbers and descriptions of your valuables. It's a good idea to place a hidden identifying mark on jewelry, watches, bicycles, cameras, typewriters, etc. Photographs also may be useful. If there's a loss, such information will be most helpful to the police, and may be your only hope of recovery or of collecting on your insurance.

HOME SAFETY CHECKLIST

1. Never open the door until the caller has been positively identified by sight, through the viewer or chain guard.
2. Put the door on deadbolt lock every time you leave, even for short periods. Older locks require use of the key to move the bolt, but some new types have automatic deadbolt setting.
3. Keep a tight rein on your keys. Detach house keys from the case when leaving your car for service. If a spare key is hidden outside for emergencies, select a place that won't be discovered, and keep it secret.
4. Don't depend on the screen door and screen windows, even in the daytime. When leaving the room, close and lock the prime door and windows.
5. Have someone at home to receive children returning from school, or arrange with a neighbor to let them in, rather than providing them with keys which can go astray.
6. Keep garage doors closed and locked at night; also lock car doors even in the driveway.
7. Light up the side and back yards at night.
8. Always put burglar alarm on alert at night, and whenever you leave the house.
9. Prevent access to your tools; place padlocks on ladder brackets.
10. Nighttime lockup includes all accessible windows.
11. Put an identifying mark or number on all portable valuables—jewelry, TV, cameras, bicycles, appliances, even furniture.

CHECK LIST FOR ENTRY BARRIERS

1. Solidly installed door locks with deadbolts of sufficient throw to deeply engage their latchplates. Doors must be in good condition, fit snug in their frames, with no space between the door edge and jamb to admit a screwdriver blade. Always double-lock the doors when leaving, as the spring latch alone is an easy mark.

2. Doors having glass panels, or with glass lights alongside the frame, are particularly vulnerable. Resurfacing with plywood panels to cover the glass may be advisable. Otherwise, use double-cylinder locks, requiring a key for opening from the inside. The key should be kept out of the lock, in a handy place that is not accessible by reaching through the opening.

Lightweight kitchen and basement doors of many homes are poorly protected with a simple mortise lock that is operated with a "skeleton" passkey. Supplementary throwbolt or doorchain is little help on a door with glass panes.

An unsafe door lock can be replaced quite easily with a rugged and efficient lock that provides double security—a slip latch that cannot be retracted because of a recessed retainer pin, and a solid deadbolt. Heavy security plate protects lock cylinder from tampering.

Door chain permits partial opening of the door to interview callers, receive deliveries, while retaining adequate protection against unwanted entry.

Stronger and more convenient to use than other types of chains, this one simply slips over the door knob. Called Door Guard, it is mounted to the jamb with four extra heavy screws. Made by Ajax Hardware Company.

3. Doors opening outward, such as found in some apartment houses, are hinged so the pins are on the outside, where they can be removed easily. The door then can be opened on the hinge side (there is sufficient leverage to overcome the short deadbolt in the latch.) Special hinges are available with pins locked in place by setscrews which are accessible only when the door is open.

4. Door chains are dependable if the chain plates are installed with sufficiently long screws that can't be yanked out by swinging the door. The lock-and-key type of chain, which can be set when leaving the house, is useful, as are barrel bolts. There also are special heavy duty steel bars and braces for doors that are difficult to defend.

5. Patio sliding doors generally have inadequate locks and may be nudged off their tracks if there is sufficient movement to clear the jamb pocket. A hole drilled through

A surface-mounted throw bolt provides added security, particularly against possible possession of duplicate keys by unknown persons. This Stanley night bolt has extra strong jamb plate.

Spring latch is a useful adjunct to the standard patio door catch, preventing the door from being lifted out of its track.

both door and channel for a heavy nail or pin can serve as a double lock. Also useful are Charley bars, or spring catches.

6. Windows at porch decks, on ground level and in basements, are difficult to protect. One simple measure is to drill small holes through the sash for nails that prevent raising the window. Various hole positions can be planned to allow opening the window part way for ventilation.

7. Built-in window locks prevent raising the sash even when the glass is broken. Keep the key in a handy place for emergency use. A more effective protection is obtained by glazing the sash with double-thickness or mesh-reinforced glass, or with thick transparent acrylic plastic which is difficult to shatter.

8. The ultimate protection for windows is some form of steel guard or gate. Basement areaways may be closed off with heavy gratings, or bars fixed into the window frames. Apartment windows accessible from the fire escape or terrace may not be blocked off or encumbered, under the fire regulations, but some forms of metal guards or folding

Vulnerable windows can be protected with steel grilles, fastened securely to the window frames. However, exit from windows facing fire escapes must not be blocked. In those locations, window guards may sometimes be used with a secret but easily opened inside latch. Make sure installation conforms to local fire regulations.

gates may be used providing they are fitted with an easily released catch. A local firm specializing in these window guards may be able to offer acceptable types, but don't compromise with fire safety to prevent burglary.

9. *Comeback for Window Shutters?* Long relegated to strictly decorative uses, the old-style window shutters may be due for a practical comeback as their value for window protection gets renewed recognition. Even in ground-floor windows, and those in apartments facing fire escapes, shutters can be a powerful barrier to both prowlers and voyeurs, while allowing adequate light and ventilation by means of movable louvers. On the European continent, particularly in Italy, France, and Switzerland, the shutters are in constant use for both privacy and protection.

Ready-made, low cost shutters usually can be cut down to fit the opening precisely. The shutters are mounted outside in pairs on hinges or swivel-type brackets, or inside the window frame. While it would appear that the outside shutters could be removed by lifting them off the brackets, that is so only when the shutters are open and folded back against the wall. When closed, however, they overlap to fit into the window recess, and thus cannot be removed short of splintering them apart. The shutters are closed on the inside with a simple latch, and they can be fitted with a burglar alarm detector for additional safety.

Interior shutters, those fitted on the inside window frame, are quite attractive and can be harmonized with the room decorations.

THE ELECTRONIC WATCHMAN

A burglar alarm system is an essential element in any home protection program. 1. The mere existence of the alarm system may deter attempts at entry. 2. If entry is accomplished, sounding of the alarm may scare the burglar away. 3. The alarm signal alerts you to the danger of an intruder in the house. 4. The alarm may bring help from neighbors or the police, and 5. Setting the alarm at night lets you know whether you've missed locking a door or window.

Obviously, the unit will do no good if it is inoperative,

either through some defect in the system, or failure to switch it "on," and may actually be harmful if you rely on it and have let down your alertness.

Thus, if a member of your household comes home later than the others and fails to reset the alarm on entering, the system is non-functional. In some instances, neglecting to set the alarm when going out "just for a little while" has given the burglars all the chance they were waiting for.

Testing is Essential. Regular tests of the alarm system are important to make sure all is in working order. The system may be in place for a year or two, even five or more years, before it is put to the real test of signaling a forced entry. Meanwhile, the tendency is to occasionally neglect throwing the "on" switch, possibly in resentment at adjusting one's actions day after day to the sensitivity of an electronic device.

A good system will have a means for easy testing of all its circuits without sounding a false alarm. Closed circuit systems nearly all have a constant "all's well" indicator lamp—even so, the bell or siren should receive a quick sound test periodically. Open-circuit systems can be checked out with a test button.

Power source is an important element in the system. The more sophisticated systems function on transformer current from the house power, with a 6-volt standby power pack, which automatically switches on if the house power fails. Other systems rely entirely on either transformer or battery power, and are thus subject to failure, or can be quickly silenced by a knowledgeable burglar.

Small, self-contained one-station alarms for apartment doors and similar locations use either a pair of 1½-volt dry cell batteries, which have a "shelf life" of 6 months to one year, or the small pencil-type batteries which have a more limited service span. While there have been improvements in design of these batteries, there always is the possibility that the alarm may malfunction when needed because of battery failure or corrosion of the terminals. Periodic replacement of these batteries is, therefore, essential. Some of the new security locks have similar self-contained battery-powered alarm units.

False Alarms Harmful. In any house with a newly installed system, the door may be opened in a forgetful moment while the switch is "on," and result in a false alarm. Repeated happenings of this kind can nullify the value of the system, since neighbors will no longer respond, and even the harassed police will ignore it. Some systems, particularly the closed-circuit type, are so sensitive that they cause frequent false alarms, usually in the middle of the night, to the annoyance of everyone. This may be caused by vibration of the doors and windows by high winds, or simply the "dropping out" of a relay. Such events soon lead to disuse of the system, and defeat its purpose.

Photoelectric and vibration detectors are subject to sounding off without reason. The open-circuit system, however, is much more simple in its circuit design and therefore less subject to false alarms.

The Family Security Retreat. What do you do when the alarm signal informs you that there's a burglar in the house? Do you rush forth into the darkness to do battle? Never! You gather the family into the room that has been set up as the retreat for such situations, lock the door securely, then try to obtain help. If you can put on the house lights before you enter the room, so much the better. If there's a telephone in the room, call the police, or shout to neighbors. Otherwise, just sit tight until you are sure all's clear. But you're ready with an escape method, should the intruder attempt to break through the inside door. If that occurs, you would still have precious moments to get your family out the window and down a rope ladder to safety, with the burglar still in the house.

4

Good Locks:
The Key to Security

Door locks are on the front line of your home security, so like most homeowners and apartment tenants you've probably worried about whether the locks on your doors are strong enough, safe enough. Perhaps you've recently changed or added a lock or two to bolster your feeling of security, but still are uneasy about the protection they provide. You've been impressed, no doubt, by what you've heard of recent technological advances in lock design and wonder whether these new locks will do a better job for you.

It is true that major improvements have been made in lock designs recently that incorporate many advantages. New concepts of cylinder mechanisms and unique key characteristics, together with more rugged construction, make these locks more resistant to picking and tampering. Stricter control by manufacturers over the key blanks make duplication far less likely. A valuable development also has been made in the formerly vulnerable spring latch by the addition of an automatic interlock that effectively forestalls the "celluloid artist" who can easily manipulate the ordinary bevel latch.

There are, in addition, a number of special purpose locks that meet the challenges of high crime areas or the need for extraordinary precaution. Among these is a bar lock, consisting of a pair of solid steel bars that slide into rugged hasps at each side of the door, a reminder of the heavy timber placed across the gates of a medieval fortress to withstand attacks with battering rams manned by hundreds. Another is a heavy rod braced against the door in conjunction with an ingenious lock, a modern-age version of the old chair wedged under a door knob.

Very likely, one of these better locks would contribute much to your safety and peace of mind. But the locks you now have may be of adequate quality, needing only a new cylinder to make them perfectly functional, or perhaps just a change of the pin tumblers for a new set of keys to give you a fresh start. Sometimes, just soaking the cylinder in a solvent bath like varnolene will restore it to proper function by washing out the grit and grease that may "freeze" the pin tumblers in the cylinder core. Another excellent step, perhaps the most effective one, is adding a second lock to each door—this doubling up has a definite value as it both reinforces the door and is one of the most positive defenses against picking. Especially important—if you don't have a good deadlatching lock, so that you know the door is always secure without further attention, that's something you need right away. The increasing incidence of daytime intrusions makes this a must.

Time for Evaluation. Before taking any further steps, it's best to evaluate the protection afforded by your present locks. It may be that some changes will be indicated, but possibly the lack of security may not be the fault of the locks you now have, or at least only partly so, and corrective action may involve factors other than the lock itself.

Have you ever thought about how a lock holds the door? You know, of course, that the lock "throws" a solid bolt that engages in a metal latch plate recessed into the door jamb. But in most common locks, the bolt moves hardly a half inch, usually even less. If there's a considerable gap between the door edge and the jamb, the bolt may be engaging the plate to a depth of only about an eighth of an inch—all that holds the door in place! It's hardly an adequate barrier, and no wonder that many a burglar has broken into a home just by giving the door a hard push. A properly fitted door, allowing just $1/16$-inch clearance at the jamb, combined with a quality lock that has a bolt thrust of three-quarters of an inch, represent a solid barrier that can hold fast against routine attack.

Another important detail is that the door jamb is usually only wood one-half inch thick, held with a few long finishing nails into a 2 x 4 wall stud that may be inches away. The latch plate is recessed perhaps an eighth of an inch deep, but there's a deeper recess beyond the plate for the lock bolt (if it ever reaches that far). It is at that very spot, at the latch recess, that the door jamb is weakest. If a pry bar can be inserted from outside between the door and jamb, only moderate force would split the jamb apart and release the latch bolt. But without the leverage obtained with an inserted pry bar, a properly installed lock can resist tremendous force directly against the door.

Stop Molding Removable. Another source of vulnerability may be seen on the outside of your door. Is your door jamb flush across its entire width so the door edge butts up against tacked on stop molding, or is there an offset in the jamb? Surface stop molding is a fragile barrier that can be easily removed to expose the door-jamb clearance. Then, if there's space enough to slip in a pry bar or screwdriver blade, the door yields quickly and almost silently because of the side leverage.

Then there is the wavering strike plate, barely held by screws that have long since loosened. The mortise, enlarged many times to adjust for a sagging door, no longer holds the plate in line, so that often the lock bolt doesn't even engage in the plate slots, and rather catches in the narrow strip of wood between the strike plate recess and the edge of the door jamb, often just a fraction of an inch of wood. Prying the door back against its hinges will free the lock bolt from this recess.

Solving Gap Problems. Here are possible solutions to these particular problems: For the gap between the jamb and door, you may be able to shift the jamb closer to the door, perhaps by inserting a strip of plywood of the required thickness, or by driving wedges between the 2 x 4 framing and the jamb, after removing the facing trim on the door frame. Possibly the threshold also will have to be lifted and cut back a bit for more clearance, before it is replaced. Be sure that the jamb is kept plumb, and test frequently by closing the door to be sure that you retain sufficient clearance.

If the jamb cannot be moved, for one reason or another, it may be possible to fasten a covering strip over the present jamb, using either solid board or plywood of the required thickness, perhaps one quarter or one half inch. Better still, use a brass or aluminum strip, attached with countersunk flathead screws.

This last procedure is the only suitable remedy for a damaged and mutilated plate mortise, provided there is sufficient space between the door and jamb to nail up. The new facing must be mortised for the plate, adding a definite plus to the door security, while the new wood will provide better holding power for the strike plate screws. In a metal facing strip, the strike mortise is formed by first drilling and then squaring the opening with a file.

Doubling the Jamb Thickness. In the case of the door with only a stop molding covering the door-jamb clearance, it is possible to increase the jamb thickness at the exterior portion of the jamb, by adding a strip of $\frac{1}{2}$-inch plywood snug against the closed door. Then stop molding can be added for weatherproofing. But the main objective, in these projects, is to remove any significant gap at the door closure.

Sticky Cylinders. A worn or grit-clogged cylinder can make any good lock ineffective. Congealed oil can cause the pin tumblers to become "frozen," that is, they stick in open position so that the cylinder core can be turned even without a key. After many years of use, the keyway can become so enlarged through wear that the pin tumbler no longer is precisely controlled by the proper key. Oil-thickened grit

What's wrong with this door? It has an old-fashioned latch and nightbolt, and a brand new mortised deadbolt, plus an interviewer chain. But that immense gap between door and jamb makes it a cinch for a burglar to jimmy it open. The lock bolts have a "throw" or movement, of less than ½ inch, while the gap between door and jamb is over ¼ inch wide, leaving the bolt barely seated in its strike plate. Just a little shove with a jimmy or heavy screwdriver, shown here on the inside to indicate direction of the leverage, will pry out the lock bolts, and the door swings wide open.

can hold the pins in the open position so that the cylinder plug can be turned with a screwdriver, which is one reason why locksmiths caution that locks should be lubricated only with powdered graphite, never with oil.

How to Switch Cylinders. The cylinder of a mortised lock is held in place by one or two very thin and long screws which enter notched recesses in the outside surface of the cylinder to keep it from turning. These screws are on the latch side of the lock, and can be removed with a narrow-bladed screwdriver. The cylinder then is free to turn, and is removed by unscrewing it from the lock housing. The cylinder body is quite deep and the threaded section covers the entire barrel,

Changing Cylinder

The cylinder is the basic element of a door lock. There are times when the cylinder should be replaced, the key code changed, or parts thoroughly cleaned for proper functioning. In entrance door-handle locksets the cylinder is secured with retainer screws, deeply set into the door edge plate. Loose retainer screws may indicate tampering with intention to turn out the cylinder. Use narrow-blade screwdriver to turn out the screws all the way so threads can be examined.

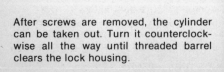

After screws are removed, the cylinder can be taken out. Turn it counterclockwise all the way until threaded barrel clears the lock housing.

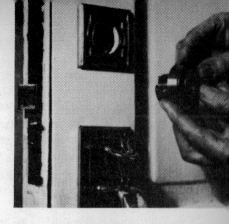

Cylinder should have a protective spring-loaded collar completely covering the cylinder rim, to prevent gripping and turning the cylinder to force it out of the lock.

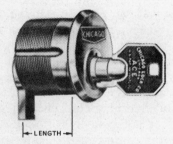

|← LENGTH →|

Slots on side of cylinder are aligned with the keyway position. When keyway is precisely vertical, the slots will line up with the retainer screws.

so it takes a bit of patience, but soon the cylinder is out. A local locksmith can examine it, clean the pin tumblers, and if so requested, change the key coding.

The "Pick Proof" Locks. Many homeowners display obsessive concern about the dangers of their locks being picked open. Actually, home burglaries that result from picked locks are quite rare, and those that do occur are mostly of apartment locks that are old and worn, in such poor condition that they could be opened with any kind of key, so really cannot be said to have been picked. An excessive emphasis on locks that resist pickers often causes neglect of more important and immediate lock problems. The most effective defense against lock picking is to have two cylinder locks, properly installed, plus an extra night bolt on each door.

How Locks are Picked. Picking a lock is done with long, needle-like steel tools, somewhat similar in appearance to nutpicks, with the tips bent into various shapes, of which

41

there are dozens. The picks are sold in sets for $10 to about $30, and anyone can buy them. An expert pick man can open nearly any lock about as easily as with a key, but it usually takes some time, even under the best conditions. Five-pin cylinders are easiest, but the wafer type also succumbs to an expert locksmith.

Two tools are used simultaneously, one the needle-like pick, the other a flat thin bar. This tension bar is inserted in the wider part of the keyway: the needle part is used to manipulate the pins. The bar maintains pressure in the direction the cylinder is to turn. As each pin is centered in position to clear the plug, it is held there by the continued pressure of the bar. When all five pins are aligned, the plug can turn, and thus move the latch bolt inside the lock. Sounds easy, but it's not. For anyone not an expert, picking a quality lock that is in good condition is an almost hopeless task that could require long periods of effort and usually without result. Business places, which are the targets of the more experienced and skilled burglars because of possible large amounts of cash on hand or salable goods, are justified in efforts to avoid any possibility of picked locks. The homeowner, except perhaps those known to possess valuable treasures or caches of cash, is less subject to this kind of menace. His lock selections, then, should be based on other factors.

Reinforcing Your Present Locks. Look at all your entrance doors now—not only the front door, but also the kitchen, rear, and basement doors, if you have any. Is there a mortise lock in these doors? If so, check the types. The front door lock, no doubt, is of better quality than the rest, and may be worth retaining, but how old is the cylinder? How long is it since the key code has been changed? How many keys to that cylinder have disappeared over the years? Does the cylinder work too freely, the key slip out when the latch is half turned, the cylinder itself loose in its housing so that it also turns partway with the key? All these are signs that the lock no longer is safe.

If there are any "lost" keys, they may be in the possession of persons waiting for a chance to make a clean sweep of your valuables, so a routine change of the cylinder gives you a fresh start with the assurance that comes with an entirely new set of keys. Knowledgeable homeowners keep an extra cylinder with keys on hand, to make an immediate switch whenever a key is lost or missing.

Quick Switch. Responding to the greater recognition of the cylinder as the core of door security, a method has been developed for re-keying of locks by the businessman or homeowner himself, privately, instantly. The U-Change Lock System, as it is called, allows re-keying without even removing the cylinder from the lock, and this change can be made hundreds of times without extra cost. The system is based on a special lock cylinder which replaces the standard cylinder in mortise locks, an assortment of extra keys, and a tumbler change tool. The cylinder plug is turned with its present key to a marked position and the change tool inserted into a tiny slot in the plug. The old key is removed and the new key inserted.

When the change tool is withdrawn, the tumblers are set in their new positions. The change is possible because the tool permits the pin tumblers to ride freely so that they conform to the configuration of the new key when it is inserted. Removal of the change tool leaves the tumblers locked in their new positions, to fit only the new key until another change is made by the same process.

The Halfway Key. If the key slips out when the cylinder core is turned only part of the way, you probably often leave the core half turned, thinking that the door is locked. But not so—anyone can open the lock merely by continuing the turn with a paper clip or anything else that will fit in the keyway. A cylinder in that condition needs immediate repair, or replacement. Similarly, a cylinder that turns when the key is not fully seated is faulty—the tumblers are frozen in the "open" position because of grit or congealed grease or other reason. Time for a change!

Updating Old Mortise Locks. The locks on all exterior doors—at the side, basement, or opening onto a patio—should

Remove knob and plate from mortise lock.

After removing two screws in the edge of the door, lock can be removed from mortise, sometimes with a little persuasion from a screwdriver in the knob hole.

be given the same consideration as the front entrance door. The "secondary" doors most likely have mortise locks, but these may be either the old-fashioned warded type that uses "skeleton" keys, or even if almost brand new, probably are "builder's hardware" which was selected for good looks and low cost rather than dependability.

Any mortise lock that has an ordinary spring latch — the kind that can be pushed back from the outside — should be replaced with a deadlatching lock. And all mortise locks should have a quality cylinder. Doors with glass panes, or nearby side panes, require a double cylinder deadbolt or deadlatch.

Old-fashioned mortise locks can be replaced with a more efficient one quite easily. Very likely you can find one that will just fit the door mortise or will require just a little adjustment. Take the measurement after removing the old lock. This is done by loosening the set screw on one of the knobs, withdrawing the knob stem, then turning out the two screws in the edge of the door that hold the lock into the mortise. The lock then can be withdrawn. Some locks have a deadbolt knob on the inside which also must be removed, which is done by turning out two screws that hold a metal plate to the door. If you have difficulty pulling out the lock, place a screwdriver against the knob stem opening in the lock and tap it sharply with a hammer to free the lock.

Take careful measurements of the door thickness, the width and height of the mortise (without allowance for the latch cover), and the distance of the knob hole from the edge of the door. Measurements should be precise, within eighths of an inch; otherwise you may purchase a lock that will require tedious chisel cutting when that could have been completely avoided by getting the exact size lock.

Installing Deadbolt

Mortised deadbolt supplements lockset, is particularly important installation for doors leading from basement, garage, or patio. Deadbolt may have cylinder on exterior side, or both sides.

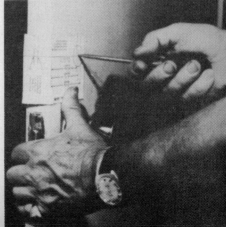

Measure from floor for convenient height, use template supplied with lock to mark for drilling on face of door and through door edge for the latch bolt. Awl or icepick makes centerpoint for drill bit.

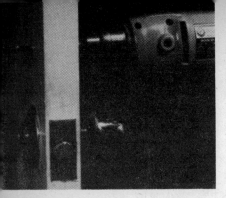

Pilot drill with hole saw drills through the marked position, hole saw automatically is centered. Pilot drill goes through the door, to guide hole saw from both sides.

Hole saw will cut through only half thickness of the door, so drilling is finished on other side. This two-way drilling avoids splintering the veneer of flush doors.

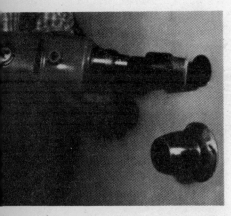

Cutting is completed as hole saw removes core.

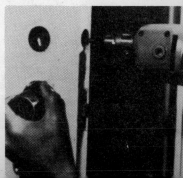

Edge of door is drilled at marked position for the bolt latch, which will be centered on the larger hole in the door face.

With bolt latch in place, outline of the latch plate is marked for mortising.

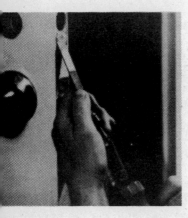

Chisel is used for carefully undercutting area to recess the latch plate. The mortise should be perfectly flat and level, so plate is flush with door edge at all sides.

Deadbolt is slipped into the door edge so it will interlock with the cylinder mechanism to form the completed assembly.

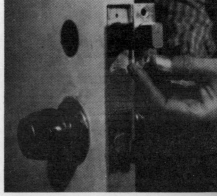

Thumbturn is fastened to interior side of door with two screws. If door has glass panes, keyed cylinders on both sides are advisable.

TYPES OF LOCKS

The Mortise Lock. The standard door lock, used all over the world, is generally regarded as the most effective for its purposes. It is fitted into a deep mortise cut into the edge of the door, and while there is but a very thin panel of wood remaining on each side, the lock generally is quite securely anchored.

One shortcoming of the typical mortise lock is that the spring latch, with its beveled edge for easy closing, is not an adequate safeguard. While the latch, when set by button to lock, must be opened by key, the beveled edge can be pushed back with any thin tool or a piece of plastic. This deficiency now has been overcome in some of the better mortise locks that include a deadlatch. This is still a beveled spring latch, but with a trigger mechanism that backs up the latch and makes it immovable in that manner.

The latch on mortise locks is operated by a cam at the end of the cylinder. The latter is fastened into the exterior face of the door by turning its threaded barrel into the lock housing. If this cylinder could be removed, the latch can be opened easily from outside with any tool. In some locks, the cylinder is retained by set screws driven through the latch plate on the inside edge of the door to fit into notches in the cylinder barrel. If these screws become loosened, the cylinder can be removed; and there are many opportunities when strangers or delivery persons waiting at the door could quickly loosen these screws unobserved. A protective metal cover on these retainer screws would overcome the defect—several locks do come with these protective plates. The use of non-retractable screws would not be practical in this instance.

A major item that marks lock quality is the "throw" of the latch bolt. The average movement is a half inch, and some even as little as three-eighths of an inch. When you consider that the door clearance alone takes up an eighth of an inch, at best, then the bolt "reach" becomes a critical security factor. Most quality locks, those rated as high "security" locks, have bolts that extend three-quarters of an inch, and the better ones will go a full inch.

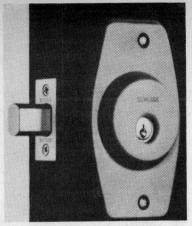

Security cover by Schlage Lock Company is an auxiliary that prevents forcing or tampering with the lock mechanism. The cover can be installed over existing lock without removing it from the door. The plate is held by four case-hardened steel bolts, two inserted from each side of the door.

Improved deadlock with hardened steel bolt pin and protected cylinder collar. This Weiser Lock Company bolt has 1-inch "throw."

So, in mortise locks, the selection should be based on the facts of deadlatched spring latch, protected cylinder retainers, adequate bolt movement, and overall ruggedness, with of course, quality cylinders.

Key-in-Knob Locks. Also known as cylindrical locksets, these have become the most popular in recent years, far outselling all other types, and perhaps soon to replace the mortise lock as standard residential equipment.

The cylindrical lock is handsome in appearance, offering individuality by selection from a large assortment of rosette surface plates (commonly called "roses") in attractive designs. The lock is convenient to use, easily controlled by a push or turn button, and the single latch combines the functions of the typical spring bevel latch and a deadbolt. The way this works is that a short deadlocking pin slips behind the spring latch to prevent its being pushed back, as could be done by a piece of flexible plastic on the older type of spring latches. All locks purchased for installation on exterior doors should have this trigger latchbolting feature.

Of additional interest to the homeowner is that the cylin-

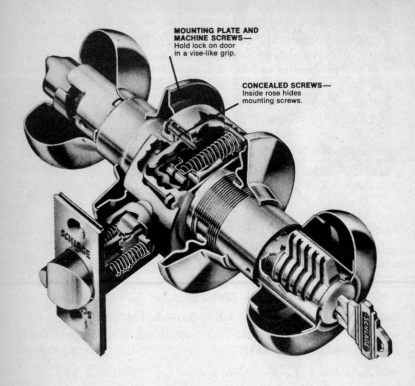

MOUNTING PLATE AND MACHINE SCREWS— Hold lock on door in a vise-like grip.

CONCEALED SCREWS— Inside rose hides mounting screws.

Cutaway drawing shows construction details of a heavy-duty cylindrical lockset for residential installation. A wide assortment of custom hardware designs in both knob and roses is available for individual selection. Lock shown is of the Schlage "A" series which has UL listing.

drical lock is the easiest to install, which means a substantial saving when several locks are to be added. All that is required is to drill two holes, one in the face of the door for the lock case, the other into the edge of the door for the latch. Then the strike plate is recessed into the door frame, a simple step. The installation is aided by use of a template supplied with the lock, and only a few special tools are needed—these can even be borrowed without charge.

Some objections are voiced against these key-in-the-knob locks. The most frequent is that the knobs are flimsy, and that they possibly could be broken off, exposing the locking mechanism. Most quality locks include a backup plate on each side, and any tampering of the knob would so distort the plate that the latch mechanism could not be manipulated. However, tests have shown that torque applied around the knob, with a tight leather strap or a chain clamp, for example, could in some instances wrest the knob or turn the latch mechanism.

Heavy duty cylindrical locks are generally of more rugged construction, and the latch usually extends at least half an inch, and in some models up to one full inch.

Maximum security from both picking and tampering is obtained by having both a cylindrical lock and a one-inch night bolt on each exterior door. Several manufacturers recognize the value of this combination and include double service locksets in their lines.

Surface-Mounted Locks. While often rejected because of bulky appearance, surface-mounted locks can provide an important extra measure of security against jimmying, particularly the vertical bolt locks which have an angled latch plate. One definite advantage is that the plate can be anchored solidly into the door frame with screws driven from two directions, while the interlocking bolt cannot be forced out of the strike plate as it can with some conventional types.

Some surface locks contain a beveled spring latch, which is locked by moving a button on the inside, and opened with a key from the exterior. Others are simply a night bolt, without cylinder. Chiefly, however, these surface locks are intended to offer an exceptionally strong deadbolt for night lockup that reinforces the regularly used lock.

Vertical Bolt Locks. Widely recognized as offering exceptional resistance to jimmying and other attacks, these locks have two vertically moving bolts that interlock with the strike plate. The lock comes with single key cylinder and turn knob on the inside, or with double cylinders for key control both inside and outside on doors with glass panes or similar vulnerability.

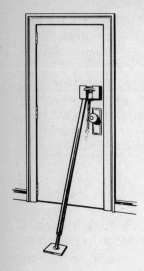

The famous Fox Police Lock features a steel bar braced against the door, making it virtually jimmyproof. When key is used in exterior cylinder, a metal block is moved aside, permitting the brace to slide upward so that the door can be opened. The bar remains fixed into a recessed floor plate, so the door swing is limited to about 40 degrees, but the brace bar can be removed from its place when full swing of the door is required.

The Fox double-bar lock, intended primarily for doors that open outward, has two steel bars that slide into hasps set into the jamb on both sides of the door. The bars are moved into position and retracted by a knob turning a worm gear in a centered gear box, or operated by a key cylinder from outside. When locked, the bars would prevent lifting the door even if the exterior hinge pins were removed. The lock can be adapted for in-swinging doors as well, using external hasp plates attached to the door frame.

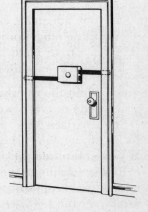

Fox Police Lock. In situations such as an old apartment, where the door jamb is weak or is splintered from screw holes of previous locks or where the door is a poor fit against the jamb, and where the landlord won't make repairs, the answer is the Fox Police Lock. This does not require any latch plate or other fitting on the jamb. The door—which must open in-ward—is held firmly by a steel bar wedged between the lock and a plate in the floor. When the cylinder is turned by the key, the bar moves aside from the stop at its end and slides through a ring as the door opens. The lock is easy to install and is strong even on an old door, because the force of attempted entry presses the lock against the door rather than straining against the screws of the latch plate as in other surface-mounted locks.

HOW TO INSTALL A LOCK

A paper or cardboard template that is furnished with most locks is essential for an accurate installation, so be careful not to accidentally discard this template. The screws provided usually are adequate, but in some situations it would be better to substitute longer or heavier screws. A case in point is when the latch strike plate is poorly anchored because the screw holes have been shifted or enlarged; with longer screws it may be possible to reach into the adjacent framing stud for a more secure fastening. When substituting screws, obtain the same diameter size, so that the head will counterset flush with the plate.

Tools Required. Mostly drills and chisels are used, varying in size according to the type of lock and the individual brand or model. Circle cutters, sometimes called hole saws, are usually needed. There are several special tools that would be helpful in making the installation and assure a correctly aligned and attractive-looking job. These may sometimes be borrowed from the lock dealer, but are not worth buying unless a large number of locks are to be installed. In that case, the considerable saving in installation cost warrants purchase of these special tools.

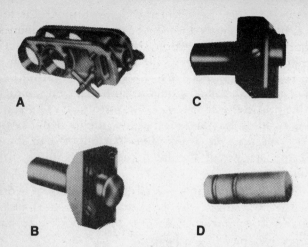

Special tools speed lock installation, assure neat result. (A) combination jig for aligning 2-⅛-inch holes in door face and ¹⁵/₁₆-inch hole in door edge; (B) latch mortiser; (C) strike mortiser; (D) dowel with center pin to mark jamb for proper strike location.

Positioning the Lock. The accepted door knob height for the average adult is 3 feet from the floor. But you may already have a lock at that position and are adding another, so the selection of position will be determined by available clearance. The additional lock should be placed above the original one, for convenience, though you may want to make an exception to this if you believe that a lock located very low, say 2 feet above the floor, will be more difficult to pick or jimmy.

There are differences of opinion about this, however, and some experts who have been consulted feel that a low lock would be even more vulnerable since the burglar would be less visible if he could sit on the floor while quietly picking the lock.

Installing a Mortise Lock. Place the template in position on the door, folded over the edge where indicated by a line. Make sure you have the correct position—the template will be marked for left-side or right-side locks, and whether it is to be placed on the inside surface or outside. Secure the template in position with pieces of masking or cellophane tape.

With an awl, carefully punch marker holes through the template for drilling, both into the door face and the edge mortise. The corners of the mortise outline should be clearly shown by the awl points.

Drill through the door face first for the cylinders and knob spindle, making the holes the sizes shown on the template. For the edge mortise you may have to drill a series of seven or eight holes with an auger or wing bit, to obtain the length needed. Draw a center line along the door edge, to guide the drill points.

A series of closely spaced $3/4''$ holes may be necessary for the mortise, drilled to a depth equal to the lock backset (width). Follow up with a chisel, clearing away the waste stock between the drillings, but do this carefully so as not to splinter the door facing. Smooth the mortise inside so that the lock body can be inserted. Press in the lock (but do not force it) so that the cover plate can be outlined, then undercut this outlined area just deeply enough so that the latch cover plate will fit in flush. Install the lock with the screws provided, two into the cover plate on the door edge, then the face plates and knob spindle, and finally the key cylinder which is secured with the thin retaining screws through the latch cover plate on the door edge.

To determine the position of the latch strike plate, move the lock bolt and close the door part way so the positions of the bolt and the latch can be marked lightly on the door trim. With a square, transfer the markings onto the jamb side, then place the strike plate so its openings are superimposed on the lock markings.

With a chisel, undercut the jamb to recess the plate flush, then close the door and operate the lock to confirm the fit. After making any necessary adjustments, use a $1/4''$ chisel to cut mortises into the jamb deep enough to receive the latch and deadbolt. Attach the strike plate with the two screws provided, after making certain that the door closes firmly against its stop molding when the latch engages.

One detail that requires some elaboration here is that of installing the cylinder. If the particular cylinder was obtained as part of the lock, it undoubtedly will be the correct size, but a replacement cylinder must be purchased to fit in relation to the thickness or "hand" of the door; otherwise it will not go in far enough, or will go too far.

The threaded cylinder is turned into the lock housing as tight as can be done by hand. Do not mar the edges with an incorrect tool; there is a special tool for this purpose used by locksmiths, but it is possible to do quite well without it. Do not use the key as a lever, as it may break off in the cylinder. If necessary insert a screwdriver into the keyway to make the final adjustment so that the keyway is vertical.

There is a useful cylinder guard with a coil-type spring at the back that takes up any extra slack and also applies tension to keep the cylinder tightly anchored. The guard has a polished brass collar that covers the cylinder rim to prevent gripping and turning it.

Installing a Cylindrical Lockset. Only two holes are drilled for this lock. Some department stores have an installation tool, which you can borrow without charge, this will speed up the lock installation and assure a proper job. Use the template provided with lock. Place it in position at the desired height on the door (3 feet above the floor is preferred). The casing hole, which is drilled first, will be 2⅛", 2¼", or 2½" diameter, depending on the lock model. This hole is centered at least 2½" from the door jamb, to allow adequate clearance for han-

With template, mark positions for drilling door face and door edge.

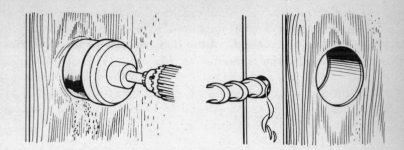

Drill face hole, 2-⅛ inches (2-inch diameter hole saw will do—enlarge hole as necessary with semi-rounded rasp), and drill edge hole ¹⁵/₁₆ inch in diameter.

dling the knob—if there is any encumbrance or other reason why the knob should be placed at greater distance from the jamb, this can be done by using a longer backset latch, which is available in standard lengths of 2⅜", 2¾" and 3¾". Extension links are available up to any desired length, permitting placement of the knob and key cylinder at the center of the door if desired.

The large casing hole is drilled with a hole saw or cutter, used with a regular electric drill, as illustrated. As the cutter can enter only to a depth of about an inch, it is necessary to drill from both sides of the door—the pilot drill bit of the cutter will penetrate completely through to the other side and will align the cutter for drilling from the other side.

Next the latch hole is bored through the door edge, carefully centered with the casing hole as indicated by the template. This hole must be drilled straight and true, in right angle alignment to the door edge. The hole will be approximately ¾" (but should be drilled to the precise dimension shown on the template, e.g. ²⁷/₃₂") and clear through into the casing hole, a depth of 2⅜" or more. Mark the outline of the latch face plate, and mortise for flush fit.

Now the lock can be assembled. With the button (inside) knob removed, put the lock through from the outside hole. When the casing meets the latch, it is manipulated so that the forked end of the latch mechanism slips into the clearance and engages with the casing.

Insert latch, mark outline of plate.

With chisel, cut mortise for recessing latch plate.

Install and fasten latch with bevel in correct position.

To do this, depress the latch tongue slightly to depress the latch fingers, and move the lock case farther in, to secure the latch firmly in position. Try the knob to test whether the latch responds correctly.

Next step is to turn the retainer plate and rosette on the threaded exterior side of the casing, pulling the plate up as firmly as possible so that the plate on the interior side can be locked on with two screws into the lock casing itself, thus providing a tight friction grip at both sides to prevent removal of the exterior rosette. The rosette on the interior side is held by some fastening device, a small spring or setscrew. The inside knob then is snapped into place.

Finally the strike plate position is located (this can be done most neatly early in the project by inserting a length of dowel, the diameter approximately that of the latch, and with a sharply pointed nail or pin at the center, into the latch bore. When pressed through the larger casing hole, the dowel point will mark the position of the bolt for the strike plate.)

There are special mortising tools available for cutting the proper depth for full lip strip, while another tool is for mortising the latch face to proper depth for flush fit. If you

Install the lock casing from exterior side, engaging the lock mechanism. Take up excess play of knob by turning on threaded shaft.

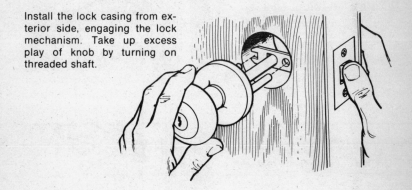

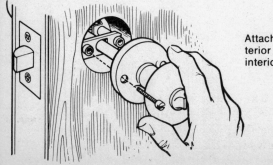

Attach retainer plate with interior screws, and install the interior knob.

Mark strike plate location.

Drill jamb for latch.

Mark the cut strike plate recess.

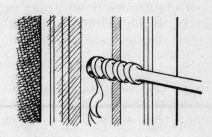

Fasten strike plate.

intend to install several locks, it may pay to invest in these tools, and possibly you can recover most of the cost by reselling them.

Modernizing With the New Styles. Now it's easy to replace a worn out and old-fashioned mortise lock with one of the attractive cylinder type locksets. Special modernization kits are available that will cover the original holes in the door faces with polished brass trim plates, while a long latch plate completely hides the old mortise opening on the door edge. You are not limited to these surface plates, however, but can select from an assortment of decorative rosettes that are available with the different brands of locks, and purchase the latch cover separately. Modernization kits, which cost just a few dollars, are made by several manufacturers, including Kwikset and Rosswin. Schlage has a special G line of cylinder locksets for installation in doors which previously had other types of locks.

How to Remove Lockset Knobs. The means by which the knobs are secured to the cylindrical lock shaft vary with the different manufacturers. There's a hint of dark secrecy about this, as very few lock brochures mention this detail. But since even the novice home burglar has learned about

This old mortise lock can be replaced by the effective and convenient cylinder lockset at right by means of a kit (this one by Kwikset) which provides fittings that cover the original openings and mortised edge. Old lock, easy to pick, had to be locked each time with a skeleton key. Lockset has thumb control that can set the door always on deadlatch.

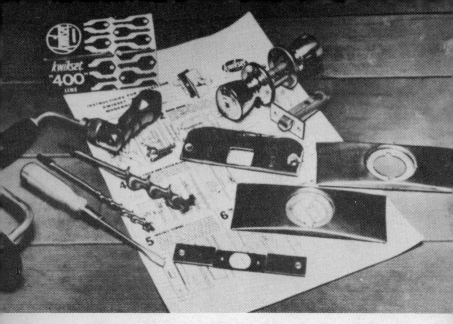

Modernizing kit by Kwikset, including the few tools needed for the changeover. Kit includes two large plates to cover the old door face drillings and receive the new lockset case, a latch mortise cover, and new strike plate with molded edge. Most installations can be done with only a set of auger bits, but in some situations a larger hole saw will be needed.

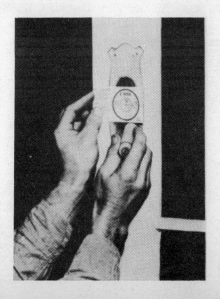

Use template to mark position of the three holes to be drilled through face of the door. The "backset" is the distance of knob stem from edge of door. The conversion usually must remain in the original backset position.

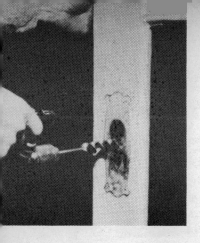

Bore two ⁷/₁₆-inch and one ⅞-inch holes at points indicated on the lock template (a single 2-inch hole drilled with a hole saw will produce the same result). Bore from both sides of the door, backing up the first penetration with a clamped board to prevent splintering the wood.

Insert the edge mortise cover in place and insert the latch all the way. If the cover plate cannot be recessed all its length, extend the original mortise as needed.

Install exterior knob and latch, then the interior knob, line up screw holes with the stems, push knob in tightly and turn in screws.

Remove old strike plate from jamb side of door frame.

Fasten new strike plate into position, after checking that it is in alignment with the latch bolt. Extend mortise as needed for fitting the plate neatly.

this almost as a first street-corner lesson, certainly there's no benefit in keeping the homeowner uninformed. For one thing, he should know to what degree a knob is vulnerable because of inadequate fastening, and for another, he should know how to remove the knob when necessary to make adjustments, or change the rosette or knob cylinder. Some outside knobs are held simply with set-screws, easily reached and removed. Most of the better locks have their knobs secured with concealed pins through the knob shank or spring-loaded retainer clips. The pin is very tiny, and can be punched out with the tip of a sharply pointed awl. But this cannot be done until the proper key is inserted into the cylinder and the knob

Tightening Lockset Knob

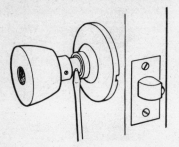

Remove inside knob by depressing spring-loaded retainer on shank with narrow-blade screwdriver. (In some makes it is necessary to force the rose inward to obtain clearance, the knob may be held with one or more screws.)

Outside knob is removed differently. First turn thumb button to lock the exterior knob.

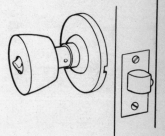

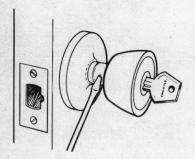

Using the key, hold the latch in retracted (open) position. Depress the knob retainer with screwdriver through the slot until the knob can be pulled off.

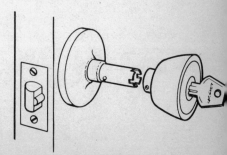

Knob released. To replace: line up slot in neck of the knob with the fitting shape on the spindle; push knob in until it hits retainer button. Depress the button until the knob snaps into position.

Unsnap the rose from the rose liner. Very loose knobs require tightening the rose equally on both sides, so the outside knob must be removed, as shown.

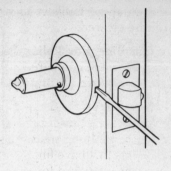

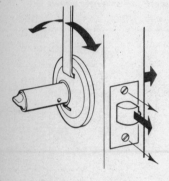

Rose liner is turned clockwise for tightening. If wrench shown is not available, a narrow-blade screwdriver can be used to turn the rose liner.

Photograph shows typical lockset with inside knob removed and the retainer slot now exposed. The rose is held in place by snapping onto spring loops of the rose liner.

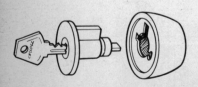

To remove cylinder from lockset handle, turn key in either direction until it can be partially extended from the cylinder plug. Then hold the knob while turning the key to the left (counterclockwise) while pulling slightly on the key until the cylinder becomes disengaged. To replace cylinder, insert key so it extends partially from the keyway, turn key to right until the cylinder body snaps into position in the knob.

turned about halfway to a certain position in which the pin can be cleared.

Installing Fox Police Lock. This surface mounted lock is easy to install compared with a mortised lock or lockset, as the accompanying illustrations show.

New Locks Meet the Challenge. Of the many innovations that have appeared in the past few years, most have been concentrated in four areas: 1. improved cylinders; 2. new keying concepts that have finally broken out of the Yale pattern which has been standard for over half a century; 3. an application of electronic controls to take the place of physical mechanisms; and 4. locks controlled by number combinations rather than by key cylinders.

Fox Police Lock is one of the easiest security devices to install. After small retainer plate is attached to floor 30 inches from the door, place the brace in it so that position of the lock can be marked. Remove lock cover by turning out two screws on surface.

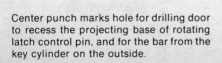

Center punch marks hole for drilling door to recess the projecting base of rotating latch control pin, and for the bar from the key cylinder on the outside.

A ⅜-inch hole is drilled from inside of door; the larger cylinder hole is drilled from the outside surface.

Fasten lock to door with four screws of adequate size, preferably 1-inch No. 12, or heavier.

Operation of lock is shown with cover removed. Brace set into floor plate is wedged into blind slot of the lock.

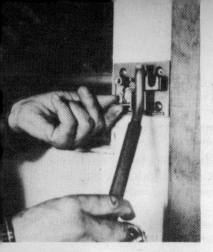

When key is turned, the brace holder slides away from the restraining block, so end of the brace is free to move.

With lock cover on, brace is shown in normally blocked position.

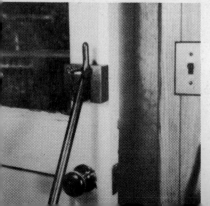

With lock shifted by key, brace can slide up inside the holder loop permitting door to open part way.

The New Cylinders. Though by no means ready to be discarded, the pin tumbler lock is being challenged by various new ideas which now must face the test of time and practical experience. One of the most exciting developments is the application of magnetic force together with the standard pin tumblers. The Miracle Lock cylinder has the conventional spring-loaded pin tumblers, plus 4 individually coded magnetic tumblers—the latter corresponding to a set of magnets imbedded into the key. When the correct key is inserted, its magnets pull free the floating pins into alignment so that the cylinder plug can turn.

A completely different approach to lock mechanism control has been taken for the Abloy cylinder, which works on the rotating disk principle. Nine of the ten disks revolve freely within the plug sleeve. The correct key aligns nine of the disks with the drop-in side bar slots so that the plug can be turned. The tenth disk is stationary, providing a bearing point

The Miracle Magnetic lock cylinder employs a combination of the standard pin tumblers with magnets. Only the correct key will release the magnet and permit the cylinder plug to turn. The key is of unique design: magnet inserts are set into dimpled recesses in positions determined by computer analysis.

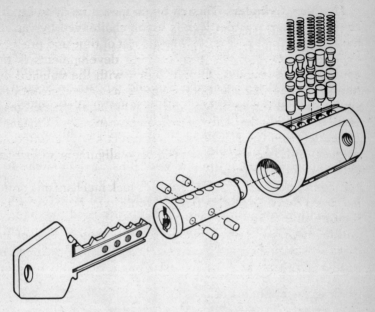

Exploded view of Miracle Lock cylinder shows placement of magnets in both the cylinder plug and in the key.

for the tip of the key as well as the cam action to rotate the sleeve.

Pushbutton Locks. The Preso-matic pushbutton combination lock has no key cylinder, thus completely eliminates the picklock hazard and is a great advance in solving the problem of lost or duplicated keys. This new lock has ten number buttons, coded into a 4-digit combination which must be pressed in correct sequence. The lock is instantly unlatched from the inside by pushing a button, allowing the door to spring open. A button, when turned as a night lock, prevents opening the door even by use of the correct number combination — an added safety feature. The locks all have deadbolts or deadlatches, and some have a spring latch that locks automatically when the door is slammed; others do not lock unless the special button is pushed. The number combination for each lock is preset at the factory, but may be changed by the homeowner at any time by inserting a new set of slides.

Dimpled Key. A completely new approach to pin tumbler arrangement and keying is the Sargent "Maximum Security System," which is not a very descriptive name, but designates a very interesting mechanical concept. Instead of the conventional cylinder plug arrangement of a row of pin tumblers which are moved into core alignment with a bitted key, the new Sargent system has three rows of pins, at right angles to each other, a total of 12 key pins in all, in scrambled sets of lengths. The key is not warded, but rather drilled for a number of shallow round recesses, on both sides and thus is reversible. The depths of the holes, determined by a computer,

Installing Pushbutton Lock

Presto! Unlock the door by pushing four of the ten buttons in a secret sequence. Door always locks when closed, but you're never locked out, because no key is needed. Preso-Matic lock shown has deadlocking latchbolt. Button at bottom clears the system so you can start over if you make a mistake in the number sequence. On the inside, one button unlocks the door at a touch. Combination can be changed by inserting a coded slide.

To install push-botton lock, template supplied with lock is placed on door at convenient height above the floor; points for drilling are marked with awl.

Edge drilling for the latchbolt is located both by template position and adjusting for thickness of the individual door. In this case metal weatherstripping along door edge had to be snipped to clear the latch bolt.

An opening 1-⅞ inches by 5-⅜ inches is required; this can be obtained by drilling three overlapping holes with a 2-inch holesaw, or by drilling a series of 1-inch holes within the required oblong area, then squaring the sides with a saber or keyhole saw.

Saber saw neatly trims excess stock. Angles must be squared to allow fitting the lock casing.

Sawed out stock removed showing the open section of required size. Where necessary, corners can be neatly squared with a keyhole saw.

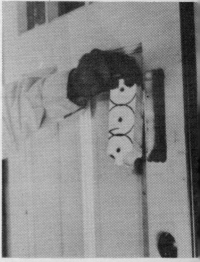

Edge of door is drilled for 1-inch hole at marked position for latch bolt. Drill must be held to go in straight at right angles to door edge so latch bolt will function smoothly without binding.

Dowel of 1-inch diameter, with pin at center, is placed in latch boring to locate the strike position on door jamb. Dowel is pressed outward from the open section.

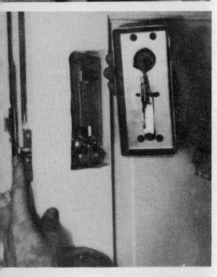

Lock body is set into the opening from exterior surface, locked into position with cover plate on the inside, at the same time engaging the latch which is inserted from the edge.

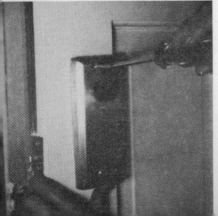

Lock completely assembled, showing the two inside buttons. One releases the latch instantly for normal exit; the other button sets the night latch so that the lock cannot be opened from outside even with the right combination.

control the repositioning of the pins so that they become aligned to clear passage for the plug.

The Sargent company says that the keys cannot be duplicated on key cutting machines now in use, and that all duplicate keys must be cut on special equipment at the plant, and are supplied only on authenticated orders of owners. There are said to be a total of 24,500 key changes available within each of seven complete master keying systems available.

Electronic Security. A new vista in entrance door control has been opened with the development of electronic locks. One of these is the Cypher Lock, which presently is used for security control in industrial plants and offices, but is expected eventually to be adapted to residential use also. The unit consists of 10 numbered buttons. As with the Preso-matic lock, a combination of four of these buttons pressed in the correct sequence will activate an electric door opener. The unit and door opener operate on low-voltage current off a 6-volt battery. An interesting feature of the Cypher lock is a "time penalty." If an incorrect or out-of-sequence button is pressed, the lock will block any further efforts to open the door (even with the correct combination) for a specified time period. The time penalty may vary from one to 10 seconds, and has the purpose of preventing repeated attempts to discover the combination by trial and error. The Cypher lock is a product of Sargent & Greenleaf, Inc.

5

Looking at
the Basement

The basement seems to be at the bottom of the list when the homeowner considers security arrangements. This area deserves, instead, the prime consideration, since it is most likely the weakest link in your defenses. It is farthest from the sleeping quarters, the doors and windows usually are of flimsiest quality, deep window wells shield an intruder from view and muffle sounds of forcing an entry, and because the basement provides hiding places, you may be unaware that an intruder has broken in until it is too late to summon help.

Cellar doors offer little resistance to entry. Almost all have small glass panes intended to provide some daylight to the otherwise poorly lighted basement area. A broken glass gives quick access to the interior throw bolt. Even without vulnerable glass panes, the basement door is a pushover. Locks are surprisingly inadequate; nearly always they are of the common mortise or rim type that can be opened with a skeleton key — or just a vigorous push!

Additionally, the hinged sash windows, so tiny that they

seem an unlikely means of entry, are an open passageway to
burglars who don't mind crawling through such openings.
Often the prowlers are accompanied by a young boy who
climbs or creeps through just such neglected spaces, then
opens the doors from the inside. Any opening that is even a
foot wide should be regarded as a possible invasion point.

Alarm Link Important. Many homes that have fairly complete alarm installations somehow fail to include the basement entryways into that system. Just because the basement
area is out of your view doesn't make it the less visible — and
inviting — to an intended intruder. Look over the entire cellar
area again with the objective of linking every door, window
and other possible entryway into your burglar alarm system
if you already have one, or your plans for a system that you
are starting to install. One big advantage here is that the alarm
circuit wiring will be much easier because there won't be any
real problem about snaking the wires or fear of damaging the
room decorations.

Basement Exterior Door. If the door has glass panes and
you want to retain them, put up a heavy wire guard over the
entire glassed area, firmly anchored so that it can't be pried
off easily, or glaze with additional panes of glass having em-
bedded wire mesh. The double glass will be more difficult
to break, and the wire mesh will, mostly, serve as a deterrent.
Better still, use sheets of transparent plastic, either Lucite or
General Electric's new product, LEXAN, which is virtually
smashproof and has been designed primarily for burglar-
proofing.

Some doors are glazed with putty around the glass, others
have wood molding as retainer strips. So be careful not to
fool *yourself* by glazing the door in such a way that the panes
can be easily removed from the outside, simply by prying off
the wood molding strips. Here's how to overcome this defect:
if the door is so built that the retainer molding is on the outside, drive a series of glazier's points all around the new glass
or plastic inserts before puttying or nailing on the molding.
The points are difficult to locate and remove, and will effectively reinforce the panes.

Plastic sheeting is a practical replacement for glass in vulnerable door panes and windows. Lexan, developed by General Electric cannot be shattered even by hammer blows. It is cut with any woodworking saw. Allow ⅛ inch clearance on all sides of sash for expansion. Leave the protective paper on until installation is completed.

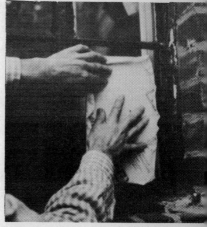

Clean sash rabbet and apply elastic putty or special tape. Fold back protective paper and press the panel uniformly into the bed of putty. Apply putty as with any pane, and remove paper. Clean any smudges with soap and water; a razor blade will scratch the plastic.

Better than doubling up the glass is covering completely both sides of the door with ¼-inch plywood or hardboard panels. This will reinforce the door itself, adding to its thickness while blocking the vulnerable glass. The light that is lost thereby can be supplied instead by installing one or more fluorescent fixtures. The 2/40s (two lamps of 40 watts each) give excellent illumination.

The plywood can be laminated to the door without clamps, using contact cement. Lift off the door by pulling the hinge pins, place it conveniently across sawhorses or other support, and remove the lock and knobs, but leave the half hinge in place. Cut the panel for each surface to precise fit, notching around the hinge leaf, and also marking the place of the spring-lock knobs on the surface of the panels. If the mullions around the glass panes are not flush, plane them down as necessary, or even remove the moldings. Now coat the door and the reverse side of the plywood panel with contact cement spread with a piece of scrap hardboard, allow the cement to dry about 20 minutes. Test for dryness with a piece of kraft paper—if the paper doesn't stick, the cement is sufficiently dry.

A large sheet of kraft paper placed over the door helps align the plywood with the door edges before the cemented surfaces touch. Place the panel on the paper, and carefully square the edges all around. Put a couple of brads part way at one end to hold the panel in place, then lift the other end and fold back the paper underneath about a third of the way. Let the panel set down in place and press firmly. Now you can remove the temporary brads, lift the panel enough to pull out the paper, and ease down the rest of the panel, which should be in complete alignment with the edge all around. Press firmly with your hands, then tap the panel with a wood block and hammer to be sure it is well bonded.

Do the same on the other side, then replace the door on its hinges. It will be necessary to adjust the door stop moldings so there will be sufficient clearance. After the door is back on its hinges, the stop position can be determined and the molding nailed back in place. Usually there is no need to adjust the door threshold. The spring lock knobs can be replaced as before, if the same lock is used, or a new deadbolt lock set into the mortise.

Better Lock Needed. The basement door warrants better locks than have been assigned there in previous times. A mortise lock with half inch latch plus an extra deadbolt make a solid combination. One of the more dependable locks for such unguarded places as the basement is the Segal or Eagle vertical interlocking bolt. Even greater security is obtained with the Fox Police Lock, or with the Kramer Double-Bar Security Lock.

The latter is best used without an exterior keyed cylinder, and usually one is not necessary for the basement entrance.

The objective for this door is a maximum protective barrier against forced entry, while retaining the means of rapid exit in an emergency.

Cellar Hatch Doors. Wood hatch doors do not offer adequate protection, no matter how carefully locked, since the wood planks can be pried up quite easily with a crowbar. Then the enclosed stairwell provides full concealment for a prowler determined to break his way through the inner door. Only steel hatch doors, securely bolted into the concrete base, provide a sufficiently strong barrier. They should best be barred from the inside. Where an outside padlock is used on hatch doors, the hasps should be of the shielded type to prevent the lock being forced apart.

Protected Cellar Windows. The extent of window protection for the basement, and the type of guards used, will de-

Apartment windows or those on lower floors of homes can be fitted with ornamental grilles, made to any size, for burglary protection. The grilles may be permanently fastened to the window frame, or one side hinged while the window is fitted with a quick release latch for emergency exit. Padlocking is permissible only where other means of exit are available.

pend largely on whether the windows are necessary for emergency escape routes. Where there are several windows, one can be selected as an emergency exit, while the others are fully blocked off. The window reserved for exit should be one that is least susceptible to attack by a prowler; that is, its location is easily seen from outside, under ample lighting at all times, and difficult to reach for one reason or another. This exit window also can be protected, but with a mesh guard that is hinged and has an easily opened catch on the inside. The other windows then can be more securely protected with fixed installations.

Flat steel bars, $\frac{1}{2}$-inch thick and about 1 inch wide, can be bolted to the window frame, spaced no more than 8 inches apart either horizontally or vertically across the window. A less expensive installation can be made with $\frac{3}{4}$-inch galvanized pipe, threaded at both ends and turned into steel pipe flanges which are attached to the frame through the flange screw holes.

Wire mesh makes a satisfactory barrier if the metal is of No. 8 or No. 10 steel wire, welded into a $\frac{3}{8}''$ or $\frac{1}{2}''$ round frame. These wire guards are available with various types of burglar-proof hinges and closing fasteners to meet different installa-

Iron bars fitted to basement window frames protect one of the most vulnerable, and difficult to watch, means of entry.

tion conditions, from local iron works or the Kentucky Metal Products Co.

Folding gates also offer a means for window security. The gates ride in top and bottom channel tracks, have riveted scissor bars with spaces of not over 6 inches when the gate is closed. Padlock fittings or cylinder locks, or a secret release catch, may be used to provide an exit in emergency. These gates are also available from Kentucky Metal Products Company.

Window Well Guards. Dependable protection of the basement is provided by iron gratings or heavy wire mesh guards installed outside over the window areaway. Essential requirements are that the guards or gratings be of adequate strength, and securely attached to concrete areaway walls. A grating of ½-inch by ½-inch bars, with welded joints, is most effective where the window is almost entirely below grade level. The grating should be installed so that the corner segments are deeply set into concrete. If the window is used occasionally for passing lumber into the basement, or similar purposes, the grating can be arranged to pivot upward at the end closest to the house wall, the front end held with a padlock accessible only from underneath.

Heavy wire mesh guarding basement window also serves as protective surface against accidental falls into the areaway. Grating consists of galvanized No. 8 wire in frame of ⅝ inch steel stock which is securely anchored to the areaway curbing.

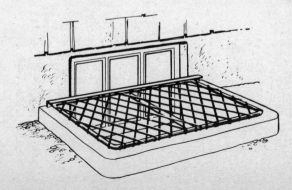

Window well gratings of No. 8 steel wire with 2-inch mesh are also practical, particularly in situations where the part of the window rises some length above ground level. The grating then can be sloped from the wall to the front edge of the area-way, with the sides similarly enclosed. These gratings, built with a heavy metal frame, are securely bolted to the areaway concrete.

For semi-circular metal wells, a new type of cover is available that offers at least some additional barrier to cellar entrance. This is a plastic bubble, made of clear Lucite, that fits over the entire areaway and covers the above-surface section of the window, with sides of ¾-inch exterior plywood. Flanges along the top and sides permit counterflashing, and the frames may be attached to the house wall with masonry anchors.

The translucent plastic does not block the light at the windows, and the covers serve also to shed heavy rains that in some homes result in flooding.

Full window guard and areaway grating of 2-inch wire mesh provides for maximum daylight in interior while serving as a dependable barrier to intrusion. The window guards are available in stock sizes or to order from Kentucky Metal Products Co. Special lugs serve as hinges for gratings that need to be lifted occasionally for passing lumber and similar materials into the basement through the window.

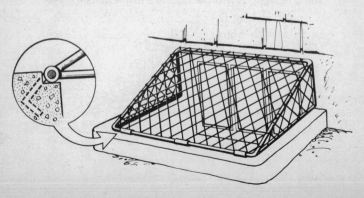

Looking at Skylights. In many urban homes, particularly town houses or "row" houses, some rooms have skylights that can be reached over the roof from an adjacent house. Any skylight is easily forced open, and it's no problem for the prowler to drop down to the floor.

Skylights have always been difficult to safeguard. One step is to see that the skylight glass is the heavy, mesh-reinforced type. Better still, replace the glass with clear Lucite plastic, at least ¼" thick, which cannot be smashed easily, or the new LEXAN plastic by General Electric.

A more effective measure is installation of wire mesh guards, either above the skylight glass, or underneath across the ceiling opening. Guards placed above the skylight should allow a clearance of several inches above the glass. For installation in the area underneath, special supports and fittings are available.

More important, include the skylight in your burglar alarm installation. One way is with aluminum foil circuit on the inside surface of the glass. This application will most likely be very difficult, however. A simpler, yet fully effective measure, is the use of trap wires strung across the ceiling opening. There also is a special uninsulated wire, No. 24 gauge, listed by Alarm Devices Mfg. Company and made especially for skylight alarm installations.

Interior Connecting Door. However carefully you've secured your basement area against entry by prowlers, don't ease up on the last but still very important barrier. That is the interior door, leading from the basement to the living area of the house, which stands as a secondary guardian of your family's safety. With all you're planning now for the basement security measures, it's important also to reinforce this door. This is particularly important in homes with an attached garage, or garage space under part of the house, from which the entry to the house is directly through this basement passage door. Once a burglar gets into the garage or basement, he can work on that door at the head of the stairs in complete concealment, using every trick in the book to break in without fear of detection. If he's sure there's nobody at home, he can use any force at all — even an ax if he finds one in the basement or garage — to crash the door, and never worry about all the noise.

A solid deadbolt latch is advisable — one with a key cylinder on the approach side if used for entry from the garage. A chain with lock attachment also is worthwhile, even though it may involve some inconvenience, though this can be minimized by reserving the chain for times when the entire family is at home. Most important is some signal to let the occupants know each time the basement door is opened — this can be a "make and break" switch which rings just once for each opening of the door, at all times of the day and evening, with a supplementary switch that throws that door detector onto the full alarm system during the night. The circuit installation remains the same as for the rest of the system, but with a 3-contact lock switch at the basement interior door so that the detector can be switched to a separate bell when desired.

6

Help for Apartment Dwellers

Apartment residents face extremely difficult and trying problems in countering constant thefts, threats to personal safety, and invasion of privacy. It would seem that apartments are easier to protect than a private home — there's just one entrance door, only a few windows (which are inaccessible except for those at ground-floor level or facing the fire escape), neighbors on all sides, and a staff of building employees at hand. Nevertheless, the amazing frequency of apartment thefts and physical assaults at all times of day and night proves that safety is not to be taken for granted. The doors and fire escape windows of the apartments are exceptionally vulnerable, while danger lurks constantly in the elevators and corridors, at the mailbox alcove, in the laundry room, the basement garage, and in an unattended lobby at night.

These dangers cannot be overcome with a simple latch or two. Rather, a whole range of defense concepts must be put into effect, aimed first at making the apartment as impregnable as possible, then at strengthening the security of the building itself against multiple dangers. The one goes with the other—you're not likely to achieve serene occupancy of your apartment in a building where doubtful characters can come and go without question, where an unlocked or carelessly supervised lobby provides convenient hiding places for waiting muggers, where dimly lit corridors are an invitation to attacks, where other tenants may in fact be the burglars you are trying to avoid, and where passkeys are under haphazard supervision.

The inescapable fact of apartment living is that the buildings are amazingly easy for prowlers to enter and to operate within at will. Do not be lulled into complete confidence because the building has doormen on 24-hour duty or all-night security patrols. These turn out to be less than reliable, at best, while service entrances are locked only late at night, the garage attendants are frequently absent making car deliveries, or busy with car washing, the stairways offer unchallenged hiding places, and the quiet corridors provide excellent cover for burglars picking a lock or forcing a door.

Tightening of the building security cannot be accomplished by the individual tenant. It can result only from the combined urging of many tenants on the building owners or management, together with the responsible participation of all the tenants in a security program. Management can cooperate by installing better locks on all entrances, keeping unsupervised doors locked at all times, paying closer attention to screening of employees, providing better lighting at the entrance and courtyards, in the lobby and corridors, keeping the doorbell annunciators in working order, assuring more careful control of the master keys, and installing window guards where requested on lower floor apartments.

All these efforts can be negated, however, if a single tenant fails to cooperate, carelessly admits anyone who buzzes the downstairs buttons, blocks a service door on leaving so it won't lock because he's forgotten the key and won't bother to go back for it, or invites crowds of barely recognized acquaintances to parties.

Armed Enclaves as Refuge? The National Commission on the Causes and Prevention of Violence in its report to the President forecast the extreme methods that would be used to assure privacy and security in high-income apartment buildings, describing the measures as resulting in "fortified cells." Some new housing developments, have, in fact, confirmed this grim prediction, placing guards at gatehouses of residence compounds like sentries at a military camp, barring entry to any visitor until clearance is obtained.

The grounds are monitored by elaborate electronic security devices such as closed-circuit television, proximity alarms, and radar detectors. While these provisions originated at very expensive apartment buildings, similar measures are now included in a number of modest garden-type developments. Carrying the picture a bit further, apartment complexes have cropped up which serve as secluded enclaves, comprising self-contained exclusive communities with clubhouse, swimming pool, kindergarten, shopping—all making for a stay-at-home existence under the protective eye of a private guard patrol. Will these places be indeed immune from criminal incidents? That remains to be seen, but experience indicates that it is doubtful. In any event, such sheltered surroundings are not available to all, certainly not to those who must work and live within, or close to, the city limits, nor would everyone choose such a closely guarded home environment. The average citizen, perhaps, is willing to accept and cope with the risks that come with more ordinary living circumstances.

Apartment Security. Apartment security calls for carefully selected hardware on doors and windows, competently installed, as a first step. Additionally, unceasing attention to details is essential, including double-locking of the door even for brief periods of absence, strict control of the apartment keys, and proper protection of the windows. The fire escape has been put there to protect you in the event of fire, but at the same time it is an ideal means from a burglar's standpoint to force his way into an apartment through the window. Remember, too, that terrace balconies on high-up floors can be scaled from the roof, or from an adjacent terrace.

How Many Locks? Pointing up the absorbing attention to the subject of door locks by so many urban apartment residents is the yarn about a woman who had an eighth lock installed on her apartment door because the previous seven had

been picked open so often. But just hours after the new lock
was installed, she rushed back to the locksmith to complain
that the new one also had been opened. The locksmith, the
story goes, suggested that if she locked only four of the locks
it would prevent the burglar from entering since his efforts
would result in locking as many locks as he unlocked.

The scheme must have frustrated burglars no end, since the
woman happily reported that from that day on, all the locks
she had locked were open when she returned home, but all
the locks that had been left open were then found locked.

This unique approach is not presented as a recommenda-
tion, but the story does point up the importance of adequate
door locks as the primary apartment defense barrier.

The lock that you find on the apartment door when you
move in should be looked at with a suspicious eye. Very
likely, the lock wasn't of a very dependable quality to begin
with, its cylinder keyway most likely so worn or gritty that
almost any key will turn it, and the lock probably is the spring-
latch type without a self-bolting feature. Then, you've no idea
as to the key situation; the chances are that an unknown number of the keys are floating around in questionable hands.
Assurances of the super as to the master key control need not
be accepted at face value. He very likely is honest and careful,
but you can't keep tabs on his staff changes.

If you are required by your lease to retain the original lock,
you certainly should insist on having the cylinder changed,
preferably for a brand new one. This still leaves the master
key susceptibility, but at least the responsibility has been nar-
rowed down. An interesting development, applying to new
apartments, is the Russwin Construction Key System. This is
a door lockset for which workmen use one set of keys during
the construction work. After completion of the building, the
first occupant receives a different set of keys to the same lock.
When the new resident uses his keys for the first time, a
change takes place in the cylinder pins that makes the former
construction keys inoperable and useless. This is accomplished by an ingenious split pin device in the lock cylinder,
and the system may end a long-standing problem concerning

possession of keys to new apartments by unknown persons who had worked on construction.

Value of a Second Lock. A second lock on the door is a worthwhile investment that practically doubles your door security. This addition which is almost essential if you're taking over a previously occupied apartment, helps make the door that much safer against jimmying as two widely separated bolts would have to be pried apart from their plates. Another advantage is that you can have two different types of locks: one for example, the conventional mortised bolt, the other a solidly mounted surface type with pickproof cylinder and double-arm bolts. Examples of suitable apartment locks are the Kwikset, Segal, Russwin, Schlage, Sargent and Abloy. These, and others that are also recommended, are described more fully in the separate chapter on Locks.

A prime requirement is that at least one of the locks be of self-latching type, so that you know the lock is set just by closing the door, even before turning any deadbolt knob on the inside, or taking the double turn with a key from the outside. Then, when you come home with arms loaded with packages, just let the door slam and you know it's locked — so important to keep an intruder from following you inside. The system works, too, when you leave the apartment hurriedly for just a brief period — to get the mail or take your laundry out of the machine — and there's the tendency to skip throwing the door bolt with your key as you leave. The self-locking provision thus provides reassuring security, keeping the door secured at all times.

You can, and should, go a step further in your lock selections. Of your two locks, one should have a deadlock bolt throw of at least $3/4''$, with a tamper-protected cylinder.

Important as the choice of locks surely is, the condition of the door itself, and proper lock installation, are two additional factors that weigh heavily in determining the strength of your defenses.

Testing the Door Condition. Perhaps you've never given close attention to the door before, but this must not be overlooked. There isn't much that can be done to buck up a sagging, battered door, with cracked stiles and warped panels, short of replacement. Many apartments have metal doors with wood filler cores. Test the center panels, since some are made of extremely thin sheeting that can be easily separated with a kick from their retainer grooves, enough for a hand to enter and shift a deadlock bolt or remove a night chain.

If the metal does not meet your test, and you can't get the door replaced, it can be reinforced with an extra panel of ¼″ plywood on the inside surface. This is not too difficult to do, and the door need not be taken down. Permission of the landlord usually is required, and perhaps also a check of local fire laws to determine whether a plywood facing would be a violation. A sheet of steel or aluminum may be used instead to good effect, attached with sheet metal screws.

Details on laminating a plywood or hardboard panel to a wood door are given in the chapter on basements. For attaching a panel to a metal door, use self-tapping screws in predrilled holes, or roundhead wood screws if there is a wood core in the door frame. Locate the screws at regular spacings to form a neat pattern.

Many apartment doors bear the scars of repeated attempts at entry which left the door edges deformed and weakened. This condition should be called to the attention of the superintendent with a request for a reinforced edging and new stop mouldings that cover any space gap between the door edge and the frame. A length of ¾″ x ¾″ steel angle iron, attached along the door edges, will add immeasurably to the apartment's security. It must be secured with non-removable screws, whose heads engage a screwdriver in only one direction. This won't be very attractive, but it will surely add to your safety and peace of mind.

Transom Treatment. A transom may appear too small for anyone to crawl through, but it can allow a prowler to reach down and unlock your door from the inside. The best thing to do with an over-the-door transom is to block it off with a solid panel, or if you wish to retain its light value, with steel bars or a heavy wire mesh guard framed with heavy tubular steel. If these measures prevent use of the transom for necessary ventilation, the alternative is to install a mercury-type alarm switch, which sounds an alarm when the transom door is tilted downward. This installation requires wire connections to a bell powered by either batteries or a transformer plugged into an electric receptacle.

In some cities, regulations require that all apartments be provided with a door interviewer. If this is lacking in your apartment, you can install one quite easily with an electric drill.

Door Chains Useful. Although you may have satisfactory locks and one-way interviewer glass to identify callers, the additional protection of a door chain is too good to pass up. Should an intruder pick the lock, or use a wandering key, the chain guard becomes an additional barrier to entry. The type

Chain with lock can be attached from outside when leaving the apartment.

Massive door lock made by 3M features a tamper alarm and inter-viewer chain. The alarm sounds when an attempt is made to force entrance or tamper with the lock cylinder. The alarm is powered by flashlight batteries, requires no wiring. Close up view of surface-mounted lock shows easy-to-use pivoted bolt control bar. This lock has extra-heavy bolt that moves almost a full inch into the solidly mounted latch plate.

that can be locked from the outside when you leave the apartment serves the double purpose of an extra lock; while an attempt to open the door while you are at home will give you additional notice and time to telephone for help. Some door alarms have integral guard chains, sounding off at any pressure put upon the chain when an attempt is made to force open the door.

Among the alarm type of chain guards are a model made by the Slaymaker Lock Company, the Alarm Lock made by Leigh Products and the Alarm Guard, product of Wessel Hardware Corporation. Also, the 3M Alarm Lock includes a heavy door chain. These use flashlight or transistor batteries.

Bolt and burglar-alarm combination is useful for apartment doors. Alarm is set when bolt is locked into the strike plate. Pressure on the door against the bolt sets alarm ringing. This Stanley self-contained unit is operated by readily available C battery. Battery must be checked regularly to insure protection.

Sliding windows, patio doors, and the like can be secured with a wraparound chain that holds against any pressure. However, it offers no protection against entry by breaking the glass.

Once the alarm has been set off, it can be silenced only by someone inside the apartment.

An easy-to-apply chain guard, made by the Ajax Corporation, is in the form of a loop that slips over the door knob. The chain is of welded steel links, brass plated, and supplied with 2-inch-long screws for solid mounting of the hasp on the door frame. No installation is required on the door itself. Standard door chains are made by Safe Hardware Company, which also produces a type called Safeguard, with a unique maze-like retainer plate that balks attempts at release of the chain from outside the door.

Sash lock prevents opening window even if glass is broken. Mounted on top of bottom sash, bolt inserts in top sash.

Sash lock slides on plate which is screwed onto top of lower sash.

Drill and screwdriver are all the tools needed to install sash lock. Place lock in position and mark for bolt hole with window tightly shut. Drill another hole vertically above at a distance that will permit the window to be locked open for ventilation, but will prevent entry.

Window Latches and Alarms. Several types of latches permit setting the window sash at various open positions, preventing further movement. Window openings should be limited to six inches. One standard protective measure is to drill a small hole in a top corner of the lower sash, and a series of matching holes in the upper sash in such a way that a nail through the holes locks both sashes in place. The nails cannot be reached from the outside when the window is open just a few inches.

There is always the danger that the glass will be smashed by a prowler standing on the fire escape. This is more likely to occur during the daytime when tenants are away at work and the street sounds cover up the noise of breaking glass. Means of window protection are limited, but you have a choice of several effective methods including metal guards, alarm detectors, and window shutters. The fire escape ladder in your building ends at least one story above the street level, approximately 12 feet, so it would seem unlikely that anyone could get up those stairs to your apartment window. This obstacle does not stop any burglar—there are ways to pull down the balanced retracting ladder so it can be reached from

Spring snap bolt for latching windows can be used on both double hung and sliding types.

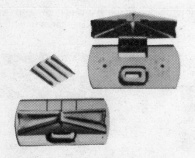

Just flip the lid and the window is secure, with this type of basic latch, which is one of the apartment security devices made by Ajax Hardware Company.

A variation of the basic snap-type window latch, also an Ajax product. This one is especially designed for sliding windows.

the street, or a simpler method of taking the elevator in the basement up to the roof, then starting down from there. Easy! On the way, a burglar can pick the most likely victims, often making a clean sweep from one apartment to another on the way down.

These windows, and all windows that can be reached from the ground floor level, need special attention. But how can those windows be protected? Keeping them shut and latched is not always practical in an apartment which has few enough windows for ventilation. Air conditioners luckily offer a great help. While they may not be placed on windows facing the fire escape, because that would interfere with emergency exits, the air conditioners make opening of windows for ventilation less necessary.

Metal Window Guards. Permanent fixed bars or a metal guard at some windows may be forbidden by the fire laws in your community, and for good reason; blocking those windows could cut off escape in the event of fire or other emergency, and also hinders firefighters from getting at the blaze quickly. However, there are some types of guards which do not present this hazard, and would be a legal installation. One type consists of folding gates with a latch that is easily opened

Typical installation of ornamental screening at lower-floor windows that are highly vulnerable to entry by intruders. The screening also serves to avoid glass breakage from vandalism.

from the inside but is inaccessible from the outside because of a wide metal plate. The Protect-A-Gard gate, manufactured by Windor Security Systems, folds out of sight into a sort of pocket when closed. The gate is quite massive and unpleasant looking for home use, however, and would be selected only where the situation is so susceptible to danger that no other means would be satisfactory.

Another type of guard that could be used at both fire escape and ground floor windows is manufactured by National Guard

Four of the many designs in ornamental treillage that can be used for protective screening of lower-floor windows and other vulnerable openings.

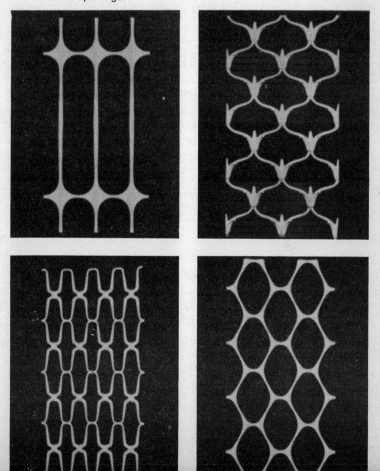

Products, Inc. Made of heavy gauge steel angles and strips, the guards come in various stock height and width sizes, adjustable for precise fit into the window opening. The guards are designed to be attached to the window frame sides with screws. There is also a way to install the guard so that it can be removed rapidly from the inside should that ever become necessary in an emergency.

This plan uses the keyhole slot principle — a larger hole is drilled immediately below and contiguous with each attachment screw hole. These holes are large enough to permit the head of the screw to go through. The screws are turned in just tight enough to permit raising the guard. When the guard is lifted only a fraction of an inch, the adjustable sections are pulled inward just enough to clear·the screw heads, and the entire guard can be taken out, without use of any tools.

The screw heads cover most of the keyhole slots so they are not visible and attempts to remove the guard are not likely, while the mere presence of the guard would act to deter any prospective burglar. Of course, for permanent installations at ground floor windows, the guards could be more solid and offer greater protection. The guards need not cover the entire window area, only to a sufficient height that they cannot be bypassed.

Window Burglar Alarms. The best solution to the problem of window security, and to apartment protection generally, is a quality alarm system. Alarm units are flexible and there are components to meet every requirement. Self-contained, one-station alarm units are of simple construction, inexpensive, powered by flashlight batteries, and easy to install. Their chief purpose is to alert an occupant to an intrusion, and that is certainly a valuable service. There are several objections to these low-priced units, chief among them being insufficient sound volume (despite the claims of advertisements), the fact that the alarm can be turned off almost instantly by an intruder just by pushing a lever, and usually shoddy construction, which makes these units not quite reliable.

Much better types are available with key lock "on-off" controls, time delay, and test indicators. A more advanced and reliable system that requires circuit wiring is based on magnetic detectors; one element is attached to the window frame, the other to the sash. The sash can be raised a few inches for ventilation, but going beyond a predetermined point will set off a loud alarm bell located in a separate part of the apartment or in the hallway.

The most effective system for window security involves metal foil strips cemented to the glass as part of the alarm circuit.

Ultrasonic Alarm. A dramatic new approach to security in apartments is an electronic intruder alarm. This is an ultrasonic device that senses motion within a specified cone-shaped area of inaudible high-frequency sound waves, and responds by both flooding the room with light and sounding a shrill alarm. The unit is completely self-contained in a wood or metal case that looks like a small radio, is installed merely by plugging into a nearby electric receptacle, and is particularly suitable for apartment protection.

The effectiveness of the unit is increased by supplementary wiring and alarm bell installations.

The unit covers a cone-shaped floor area of 100 and more square feet (depending on the model or type). A lamp cord is plugged into an outlet of the alarm cabinet. When any person moves into the area of the ultrasonic beam, the unit first switches on the light – which can have a startling effect on an intruder. After 15 seconds delay, the alarm siren goes on. The time delay has two purposes: it adds a surprise effect to scare off an intruder, but also gives the occupant an opportunity to shut off the alarm if the switch has been tripped inadvertently or it becomes necessary for the occupant to cross the controlled area.

The housing of the device has terminals for connecting a remote bell or horn with low-voltage wires, and the alarm siren itself can be silenced. Thus, when the alarm goes off, the intruder would not be able to trace the source to the alarm box, since that is not distinguishable by appearance. If desired, the remote bell may be located outside the apartment, possibly in the hallway, if that would bring help.

If you attach a remote bell to the unit, the bell should operate on its own 6-volt lantern-type battery, and have a constant ringing drop relay on the line. Thus, even if the intruder quickly finds the alarm box and unplugs it, the remote bell will continue to sound, on its own power source. If this bell is placed high on a hallway wall, or in an adjacent apartment, or some other location that can't be reached easily, it will provide maximum effectiveness in scaring off the intruder or bringing previously arranged assistance, possibly from the building staff or neighboring tenants, or notification to the police department.

Typical of these ultrasonic alarm units are:

3M Intruder Alarm, by Minnesota Mining and Manufacturing Co.

Sears Roebuck Ultrasonic alarm, with separate horn (may be used as central alarm station with window and door detectors).

Theft Prevention Company, Ultrasonic Alarm.

Delta Products, Inc. Deltalert, plus horn.

Bourns Security Systems, Inc. ultrasonic alarm.

Emerson Electric Co. (Rittenhouse) Alert-Alarm unit.

Shutters Coming Back. One additional possibility for window protection is the use of hinged louver shutters, installed either on the outside or inside window frames. Such shutters are widely used in France, Italy, and other European countries for both privacy and security. The shutters are conveniently opened and closed from the inside, and the louvers are adjustable to provide plenty of light and air while barring prying eyes.

Wood shutters are the most frequently used. They can be purchased ready-made in pairs at any lumber yard, and can be planed down for precise fit. Aluminum and steel shutters of this type are also available. For outside installation, the shutters are hung on pivot hinges attached to the house wall or to the window frame. Inside shutters, easier to install and manipulate, are quite popular for their decorative effect. A sturdy but easy-to-use inside latch can be attached to lock the closed shutters. A flat steel bar placed across the shutters in retainer brackets will provide additional security.

Elevator Manners. Apartment residents coming home late in the evening must pass two hurdles before finally reaching their apartments. These are the lobby and the elevator. Apartment house lobbies are notoriously easy for anyone to enter. The main door lock usually has become so worn from continuous use that it can be opened with almost any key, inserted just far enough to turn the cylinder, or even with the edge of a dime. It's up to the tenants to see that such a lock is repaired or replaced.

Entry often is gained by pushing someone's bell, mumbling into the annunciator, and waiting for the click of the door release. In most buildings, even those with tight security at the front door, little attention is given to other means of entrance such as the basement garage. Most apartment garages are unattended, poorly lighted, and there are vast spaces from which hidden muggers can spring upon unwary arrivals. The garages also provide a means of access into the building through corridors or elevators reaching the garage level. One measure to deal with these problems is the installation of electrically operated overhead doors at the garage entrance, controlled by key or radio signal. This is effective only if the tenant driving into the garage closes the door immediately—if he waits until he has parked the car, someone can easily slip inside. Automatic, self-closing doors with photoelectric controls only partially overcome this deficiency. Attempts to solve the problem of elevator access by locking the elevator doors and closing off the stairways make it necessary for tenants after parking to walk around outside to the front lobby, and some object to this. Keys to the elevator doors may be the next step in this security measure.

Prowlers hanging around inside a darkened lobby are bent on robbery. Tenants can insist that the lobby be well lighted at all hours. That will reduce the possibility of intrusions and permit a quick reassuring glance by the tenant returning home to determine whether there is any unfamiliar and suspicious-looking person loitering there.

If the lighting is not at the usual level, take it as a warning. It would be best to beat a temporary retreat, find a telephone and call either the superintendent or someone of your family to meet you in the lobby.

A small whistle may be some defense. Easily held in the hand, it could be used quickly if an assault is threatened — a sharp blast on the whistle may well drive away an attacker, and likely will bring neighbors to their doors to investigate.

Before entering a self-service elevator, hold the door a moment while you look to see who may be there. Nearly always, any additional passenger will be a neighboring tenant whom you will recognize. Many elevators are fitted with a mirror to reveal any person attempting to hide out of sight in a corner. If there is a stranger, and his appearance makes you suspicious, just back out and let the elevator go. If you do enter, move immediately near the control panel and notice the location of the alarm button. At any untoward move by the other occupant, you should be ready to press — and keep pressing — this button to summon help. While assistance possibly would be slow in reaching you, the mugger may fear that sounding the alarm can trap him in the building, so will most likely decide to make his escape pronto.

If you find yourself in an elevator with a suspicious-looking character who gets off at the same floor you do, and follows down the corridor, don't open your own door, but rather ring the bell of another apartment. The intruder may well respond to this by fleeing down the stairs. Of course, it may turn out that he was just visiting another tenant, and thus had a right to be there. Your embarrassment at disturbing the neighbor may be covered up with some little excuse; for example that you were expecting a package delivery and wonder if it had been left there. You might tell the truth about what happened, and that's certainly a lot better, but it's a gambit that you can't repeat very often.

Certainly there is no easy answer to the dangers that lurk in unattended lobbies and elevators, particularly late at night. Temporizing with various devices may get you out of trouble on occasion, but the better part of valor is to make more reliable arrangements. A good watchdog is an excellent companion on walks, a dependable assurance against being taken by surprise in a darkened street. Less effective is a small pocket-size alarm that can be held in the hand, which emits a continuous siren sound that will very likely frighten off an attacker. And if the hazard of late hours makes you decide to come home earlier, that is just another of the adjustments required in this high-crime period.

Central Office "Hot Line." Direct burglar alarm connections to central office stations have long been used for protection of offices, stores and other commercial places. Recently, because of the increasing burglaries and the greater concern for security by citizens living in high crime areas, central office service has been extended to cover apartments as well. The Holmes Electric Protective Company now provides an apartment intrusion detection service which combines a monitored door alarm unit and 24-hour armed guard assistance. The equipment consists of a control box with an on-off switch operated by a special key. You leave the unit "on" when you are out of the apartment, or are alone or asleep. If an intruder enters, a signal light flashes on the monitored control board and uniformed guards are rushed to your apartment from a nearby guard station. In addition to the door detector, a remote control button can be installed on a bedside nighttable, or other location in your apartment which can be used to bring prompt assistance in the event of any danger, or other emergency such as sudden illness. The Holmes people say that the mere presence of their Holmes Seal on the apartment door has reduced the incidence of burglaries in the protected apartments. However, a series of forgetful door openings, without first disconnecting the alarm switch, will bring an embarrassing rush of armed guards to your apartment. If this happens more than just once or twice, you might find the response less prompt after that.

What is best to do when you awake during the night and have a suspicion that someone has broken into your apartment? The safest action usually is to play possum, pretend that you're asleep, and hope that the burglar will leave you alone after he has filled his pockets. But that depends also on certain things. If the intruder definitely is in another room, and you can move without being spotted, and if you have a lock on your bedroom door, then you might try sneaking quietly out of bed to reach and slam the door shut, then instantly throw the lock bolt. The situation then has changed, and you have at least a few minutes to attract attention. First try to use the telephone to call police, screaming all the while for help. If you think the burglar will make an effort to crash the door, roll the dresser and other furniture up against it — each piece adds that much to the barrier.

Banging on heating pipes, screaming out the window, rapping the floor with your shoe heels, all can cause a considerable amount of noise and disturbance at night, something no burglar is comfortable with even though he may have taken his own precautions by determining that no one else is in the building, that your telephone is inoperative, that there's no alarm system, etc.

While there's always a chance that the prowler may be a violent maniac, it is unlikely. The odds are that he has broken in for the purpose of theft, and is anxious to get away quickly. All the time that he is there you remain an easy victim for assault, and any panicky, poorly timed move can arouse a violent response. So your attitude must be pragmatic — taking the step that gives you the greatest chance to escape injury in the particular circumstances. If you live in a building where there are friendly neighbors on whom you can count for help, and you're sure there's someone nearby, then an effort to get their attention would be justified if it can be done with at least temporary safety. If you can use the telephone surreptitiously, dial your local emergency police number, usually 911, or dial operator and say "emergency," then give your telephone number, your address, then name or apartment number, and finally whatever information you can about the situation, all in that order.

Laundry Room Safety. An especially troublesome part of apartment living is the laundry room. Usually located in the building's basement, where there is little supervision over comings and goings through the service entrance, the isolated laundry room has been the scene of numerous robberies and personal assaults on women attending their washday chores, often entirely alone in a vast room. Many apartment managers now limit the laundry room schedule to just a few hours a day, at the same time maintaining a closer security watch including use of closed circuit television, and the result has been a considerable lessening of crime incidents. Recent building designs provide for smaller laundry rooms on individual floors, or alternate floors, and this is much preferred as it eliminates the basement trip and shortens the time that the tenant is away from her unguarded apartment.

Wherever possible, women using the laundry should arrange to go in pairs, but this is a difficult arrangement for busy housewives to make. Every effort should be made to avoid remaining alone in the room for longer than is necessary to load the machines.

7

Family Security Room

If you are awakened and have reason to believe that there's a burglar in the house, what do you do? Certainly it would be worse than foolhardy to sally forth to investigate and perhaps give battle with an intruder, single-handed in the dark, not knowing where he may be hiding, whether he is armed, how desperate he is, what he is after.

A practical answer to such emergencies is provided by a "security room" which has been set up as a second line of defense. Just having such a retreat available will add to your peace of mind, and in an emergency, may be life-saving.

Whenever endangered, if you can't get out of the house, quickly retreat with your family into the security room, putting a solid locked door between you and a possible attacker. In this way, you will avoid emotional panic and ill-considered actions, which sometimes are more responsible for tragic consequences than the original cause of an emergency. Specific planned procedures, to be followed when danger threatens, are an invaluable safety measure.

Selecting the Room. These security arrangements would not in any way affect the usual, everyday use of the room, nor need they require any basic alterations or extensive equipment. The first step is to select the room that would be most advantageous. Since a dangerous situation is more likely to occur at night, a bedroom is the best choice, especially in two-story homes. This room should be central to the other bedrooms, those occupied by children or elderly persons. The "master" bedroom usually is the most logical one, since it is the parents who would respond to and take command in a danger-threatening situation. Any of the other bedrooms that are too distant to the central plan can be fitted with their own protective locks and communication or escape equipment.

In apartments, things are more compact, with less distance between you and an intruder who jimmies the door or a living room window, and also less space in which you can maneuver. The function of a secure room still could be utilized as stated above, if the bedroom door can be locked swiftly and smoothly. A bathroom also may be suitable, particularly if it has an outside window that can't be reached from the fire escape, but you should not count on always being able to slip to safety from the bedroom without being intercepted if the intruder is in the next room.

Setting Up the Room. The essential detail of the security room is a dependable door lock that will function instantly, since locking the door might have to be done in a race with the burglar before he can get into the room. The old-style mortise lock, with which most interior doors are fitted, usually isn't adequate for this purpose; its "skeleton" type key works haphazardly at best, and tends to fall out of the keyhole, so it may be missing when needed. Securing the key with a chain or twine may hamper turning, and keeping the key on a separate hook will mean loss of time while fumbling it into the keyway.

An improvement, leaving the original lock intact, would be to replace the key with a fixed turn knob that comes complete with a new escutcheon plate. This knob is easily installed, and the cost is nominal. Such a unit is manufactured by the Safe Hardware Division, Emhart Corp., available at most hardware stores. A separate mortise latch bolt, the type that is recessed into the door, is the most favorable solution. The Sears model, with key cylinder permitting the locked door to be opened from outside, or without the cylinder, are suitable types. Standard exterior door locksets are even better for this purpose, requiring just the turn of an inside button to deadlock the door.

Reinforcing the Door. The condition of the door is important. The stronger the door, the more positive will be the safety precautions. If yours is a lightweight panel type, less than 2 inches thick, consider reinforcing it with an additional panel of $1/4''$ or $1/2''$ plywood, laminated with rubber cement. This extra thickness stiffens the door, makes a great difference in the resistance to attack, and has an added value that you will appreciate in its sound insulating qualities, making for a quieter home. One drawback of the laminated paneling, however, is that the plywood edges are exposed. This has been overcome satisfactorily by the use of wood filler and paint, or by covering that narrow edge with metal channel moulding. Make sure, also, that the door frame is in solid condition, the latch strike plate securely attached to the jamb, and that there is no open space between door and frame that would permit inserting a screwdriver or prybar.

When the reinforcing panel is laminated to the outside face of the door it will be necessary to shift the position of the door stop mouldings. This step will not be required if the panel goes on the inside surface.

The room should have a window facing the street, possibly one that permits an easy exit in the event of emergency, by some means such as a rope ladder. Another important detail is to keep an extra front door key in the room so that you can toss it down to police officers or others coming to your aid, thus facilitating a quick search of the house.

Avoiding an Attacker. The strategy is to bring your family into the room as quickly and quietly as possible, and immediately slam and lock the door. It will also help to push a heavy dresser or chest against the door; the burglar is unlikely to crash this unless he is after a specific item about which he has some information, perhaps a particularly valuable piece of jewelry. But meanwhile, you have your own options to forestall further invasion and attack—you can try to get help, sound an alarm, or make your escape.

Use the telephone to call police or neighbors for help. If the phone is not working, you then resort to whatever means are available—which should have been decided upon beforehand in planning the security room—to arouse nearby neighbors, who would call in the alarm and come to your aid. A whistle, or just shouting, can achieve the desired results. Remember that raising a rumpus, while you have the chance, may be enough to drive the intruder away.

An electronic bullhorn, which has a sound range of over 300 feet, is an excellent and handy device, obtainable from Lafayette Radio. The D type batteries operating the horn should be replaced periodically to assure full volume of sound. Another effective attention-getting method, which is generally overlooked, is the use of firecrackers. The boom of a cherry bomb at night could wake the neighborhood and scare the daylight out of any nighttime sneak. Just a string of tiny crackers also would do the trick even where houses are situated quite far apart, since their machine-gun staccato carries well at night and is not likely to be mistaken for other sounds. The firecrackers can be set off harmlessly outside a window if a suitable bracket is available to hold them in safe position. It's just a detail, but a significant one – make sure there's always a book of matches conveniently placed in the room to set off the firecrackers.

Youngsters often connect up sending and receiving tickers with low-voltage bell wire to adjacent houses of friends, for Morse Code practice. Such a linkage, which usually has call bells at either end, can be very useful also for adult communication when an emergency arises.

Panic Button. Another effective device is the panic button, sounding a siren or automobile horn located somewhere outside the house, under the eaves. A horn obtained from a second-hand or dismantled car can be easily hooked up to a transformer with a low-voltage bell wire. Also, any house alarm system with a central control box and separate bell or siren can be wired to include a manually operated switch, similar to a doorbell button. Pressing the panic button actuates the alarm even though the burglar has managed to disconnect or bypass the other sections of the alarm system, if the panic button is wired directly to the bell circuit. A similar panic button is included in central service systems such as those provided in certain cities by the Holmes Electric Protective Company and the American District Telegraph Company, over leased telephone lines. Several such buttons may be included in a home system, with one button located in the security room.

Distress Signals Helpful. With the vast increase of burglaries and personal assaults, many cooperative neighbors have developed ingenious methods to signal distress and a call for help. One instance of such neighborly communication that attracted much attention in the newspapers at the time, and had a happy ending, involved a manager of a suburban branch bank. Early one morning, three armed gangsters broke into his home as part of their plot to rob the bank. Leaving one of their number to hold the wife and children at the point of a gun as hostages, the other two bandits forced the bank manager to drive them to his bank, open the vault and hand over sacks of money. But meanwhile, the next-door neighbor, a New York City policeman, had noticed a pre-arranged signal in the family's breakfast room. The neighbor unhesitatingly phoned local police, who rushed to the home and subdued the gunman there. Quickly surmising the full situation, the policemen called their headquarters and patrol cars were rushed to the bank, arriving just in time to grab the two bandits.

Lighting Up. Lighted rooms and hallways are to your advantage, so throw on all the light switches you can while dashing into the security room. Of course, the burglar can turn off the lights, or smash the bulbs, but light may drive him off. It is still better if you have the modern low-voltage switching system with a master control in the security room. This permits turning on all lights, including the backyard and driveway floods, and also the basement lamps, from the central control switch. Lighting up the security room also will make you feel more confident, and the fully lighted house will help attract the kind of attention that any intruder tries to avoid.

Wait Patiently. Once in the locked room, how can you check whether there actually is a burglar in the house, or whether he is gone and the coast now is clear, so that you can safely leave the room? If you've managed to alert the police and they have made their usual search, you can feel confident that the danger is over. The police are experienced in sizing up the possibilities, know where to search for a possible prowler, and will not leave the premises until they are satisfied that all's safe. If there has not been any checkup, it would be better to patiently wait it out behind the locked door as there may not be any safe and sure way to check. Resist the inclination to open the door and peek, as the intruder may be waiting nearby just for that opportunity. When you do come out, don't feel annoyed with yourself if it all turned out to be a false alarm — it's more intelligent to act on suspicion than to ignore it until there is a dangerous confrontation, when it would be too late to protect yourself. Nor should one or two false alarms make you less responsive to any new possibility of danger; on the contrary, the one time you relax normal caution may be critical. The better attitude is to regard the initial responses not as jittery flights, but rather as trial runs, each one making you more capable of dealing with any real crisis should one occur.

REQUIREMENTS FOR A SECURITY ROOM

1. A solid door with a quick-functioning deadbolt lock on the inside.
2. Window or other means of emergency exit.
3. A means for climbing down safely, by easily-attached fire escape ladder or permanently anchored knotted nylon rope with hand grips.
4. A telephone, preferably a direct line, but an extension will do.

5. A secondary means of signaling, if the telephone does not work, such as hand-operated siren, loud whistle, fire-crackers, bullhorn.
6. A fire extinguisher. Foam type, which is suitable for any electrical fires.
7. Ideally a master switch on low-voltage relays controlling all the house lights, or at least the outside floodlights, which would be turned on to help police nab the intruder.
8. A front door key in the room to let in police.

FIRE PROTECTION

If the fire warning signal is sounded, the recommended procedure is to immediately guide your children out of the house, and stay outside. If your exit is blocked by flames or smoke, then take the children into the security room, shutting all doors on the way, and leave by the window using your stored ladder equipment. If there is time, put in an emergency phone call to the firehouse, otherwise make the call from an outside alarm box or a neighbor's telephone. Don't delay your escape to gather up any clothing or valuables — it's dangerous.

The fire extinguisher is not intended to encourage you to fight the fire alone; however, some small fires may be caught at the very start, before they have had a chance to spread, in which case the use of an extinguisher may be warranted and may succeed in quenching the fire before much damage has been done. Even so, the fire should be reported to the fire department, which will take proper steps to make sure that the flames will not flare up again. Many a small blaze that seemingly had been extinguished turned into a major fire after smouldering undetected for hours.

Leaving by the Windows. Compact folding escape ladders have been developed for quick and safe emergency exit from a window. One all-metal type made with steel chain and aluminum rungs, has tubular brackets that are instantly and securely settled over any window sill. Tubular spacers steady the ladder and hold it away from the house wall, making for easier and faster descent, even for persons who would be nervous on any ladder. This ladder, rated to hold 1,000

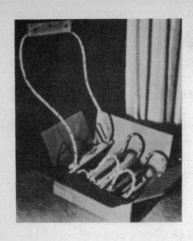
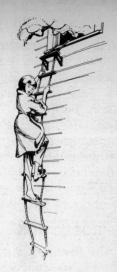

Emergency ladder should be kept secured at window and family should have drill in its use. It will hold several adults at once. It packs neatly in its own case.

pounds, enough for two or more persons to descend simultaneously, is available from Spartan Sales Co. or J. & P. Products Corp.

The ladder rolls up into a small bundle for storage and easy access. In use, the support bracket is slipped over the sill, and the ladder simply allowed to drop down providing easy accessibility in emergencies.

A true rope ladder, made of marine rope with oak rungs, is offered in the 14-foot length, enough for most two-story house windows, by Hotchkiss Products Co. Nylon strap and rope ladders, fitted with 1¼" aluminum rungs through which the side straps are threaded, and with attaching loops at the top, are available in any length on order from Rose Manufacturing Company. The nylon ladders are lighter, more compact when rolled up, and stronger than those made of hemp, and are not subject to deterioration when stored for long periods of time – all important details to be considered for emergency escape ladders.

THE SECURITY CLOSET

Always considering that an intruder may get into your house despite all precautions, you can still stay a jump ahead in

Security closet houses safe for valuables and also provides shelf space for guns and other dangerous articles that must be kept out of reach of children. Interior walls should have wire lathe and two layers of sheet rock.

protecting your valuables by providing a specially planned security closet. The security closet, an auxiliary part of the security room plan, is fitted with a built-in wall safe, filing cabinets, and specially arranged shelves and drawers to keep jewelry, reserve cash, stocks and bonds, important documents, and such valuables as fine silver, art objects, expensive furs. While some of these items belong in a bank safe deposit vault, the fact is that often several of them are brought to the house for one reason or another and are vulnerable to loss. The security closet also will be useful for storing guns and ammunition, fishing reels, and dangerous medicines or chemicals, all safely locked out of the reach of children, and doubly protected from loss by fire or theft.

While the closet could be set up anywhere, it is best located in your combination bedroom and security room, thus removing your most valuable possessions from areas where they would be quickly found. The back part of a walk-in closet would be highly suitable for this, if the space could be spared. Often, a new closet can be built recessed into a wall that backs against the roof eaves, thus providing additional storage space.

Specifications recommended by the Schlage Lock Co.,

Wall-mounted safe can be set into a closet from the rear or from a side wall, fastened through the metal flange at top.

The door of this safe is recessed so the combination lock knob is flush with the surface, permitting the safe to be completely concealed behind a picture or other means of surface covering.

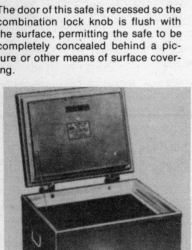

Lid-type safe box can be set into a cabinet, or even into the flooring for greater concealment. Safes are rated for fire resistance, with Underwriters' Laboratories or Safe Manufacturers National Association rating label. Desirable for protection of safe contents is a rating of 1,700 degrees for one hour.

are for walls of ⅝ or ¾-inch gypsum board over metal lathe, a metal class B door frame, a solid-core class B door 1¾ inches thick, with 4½ x 4½ inch hinges having nonremovable pins, also an automatic door closer, and two Schlage locks, the A80P0 with ½-inch throw, and the B-460P, keyed alike. In planning the construction, do not overlook the fact that closets have four sides, and that often the side walls are weaker than the door. That is one reason for the metal lathe, which is most tenacious stuff to break through, in addition to having extra fire retarding properties. Double-thickness gypsum walls are recommended, one layer placed vertically, the other nailed and glued across, horizontally.

A small, fire-rated safe is built into the wall for jewelry, cash, deeds, securities, and other papers. Such safes are available from Mosler Safe Company, the Schlage Lock Company, Marvin-Hall, and others. A low-cost asbestos-lined safe is available from the Nor-Gee Corp. A Sentry Personal Safe, 17½ x 24 exterior dimensions, with 3-number combination lock, is available from the Accountants Supply House.

If a safe is not enclosed in wall or floor, it is best to disguise it. This model is an attractive night table.

A round safe placed into the floor may escape attention, particularly if covered with carpeting. When encased in cast concrete, which can weigh 1,000 pounds and more, the safe will be virtually immovable and most difficult to attack in the floor situation. Such floor safes, as illustrated, are manufactured by American Security Products Co.

Hiding Places. A clever hiding place is often a better defensive measure than the most burglarproof lock and safe. If for any reason you will not have a security closet, there are many suitable hiding places around every house or apartment that can serve the same purpose. Your ingenuity can be put to work devising some secret place of your own, including such possibilities as false ceilings in clothes closets, slide out wall cabinets with space behind them, spaces between ceiling joists in the basement or attic, removable floor boards or tiles, with spaces between the floor joists.

But don't fall into the error of stuffing valuables into cubbyholes with just wrapping paper or envelopes. More than once this has led to tragic consequences when a plumber or electrician, doing some work in the house, came upon the bundle and discarded it because it looked unimportant. Best to place such items in special containers, such as metal bond boxes, which always have a small lock.

ARMS AND THE HOME

One consequence of the soaring number of home burglaries has been the purchase by many homeowners and apartment residents of various weapons, including firearms, for self-defense. Angered and at the same time frightened at the thought of a sneak thief breaking into the home, they obtain the weapons with a determination to resist, and of course defeat any intruder. But these arms purchases are made frequently without adequate regard to the many factors involved: whether the persons in the family who might have access to the guns, or might be called upon to use them in a crisis, have the personal capacity and experience to do so safely and effectively; whether the particular weapon is suitable to the

Round floor safe installed in concrete or into a wood floor offers excellent burglary protection and fire resistance.

Safe to be encased in a cast concrete block with welded steel casing, for installation on the floor. Concrete alone weighs over 1,000 pounds in 30-inch height, 22-inch sides. Safe may be bolted to the floor with special anchors.

intended purpose, and also whether having such weapons handy in the home might spark unpredictable and tragic accidents. The last item is as urgent as the others, since personality traits have a heavy influence; quickly aroused tempers sometimes prompt unintended resort to weapons on matters that would otherwise tend to cool down of their own accord. Inept handling of a gun when confronting a prowler may provoke a retaliation causing injury or death that might have been avoided. Your best hope is that the burglar is anxious to make his getaway as fast as possible without inflicting bodily harm.

A study by the National Commission on the Causes and Prevention of Violence reported that there are presently about 90 million firearms in private possession in the United States, and estimated that "about half of American homes have a firearm." Other estimates put the number of such weapons as high as 200 million, of which probably a fourth are hand guns which are easily concealable.

To arm or not to arm? That is indeed a difficult question. Experienced law enforcement authorities strongly advise against trying to attack or capture a burglar in your home, unless you are experienced in handling firearms and trained in apprehending criminals. Avoidance is clearly the best defense. The safest course is to concentrate on secure barriers and alarm systems, to keep intruders out, retreat into a locked room should a prowler manage to break in, and stay there until you're sure all is clear or police help has arrived.

You may confidently believe that you would be able to get the jump on a prowler unawares, putting him out of commission with a well-placed shot. But can you count on events working out so perfectly? It usually turns out the other way around, with the intruder having the advantage. Don't think the nervous burglar will stand around waiting to be cornered. You can't possibly remain on guard around the clock. The sounds of forced entry that may awaken you will be too late, and what about stealthy breaking in that you won't hear at all? In any event, the burglar may be also armed, more aggressive and desperate than you are, ready to spring from some unexpected spot or take a shot at you first if he's endangered.

The only favorable light on the subject is that the number of robberies in the home, which means burglaries involving physical attacks, is relatively small. In most cases, the burglar is just as anxious as his victim to avoid physical encounters. The thief wants to grab up what he can, and get out as quickly as he can.

But what if you are taken by surprise, while away from your bedroom investigating a suspicious sound, or some similar circumstance? In that case, you have no choice other than to cooperate with the demands made on you, handing over your cash and jewelry, or revealing where they are kept, quietly, without making a fuss.

Your best hope is that the robber is anxious to avoid inflicting bodily harm, which would land him in greater trouble if he is caught. But you can't depend on that. Many householders have been mercilessly beaten and pistol-whipped, sometimes because the robbers were not satisfied with the loot they obtained, or they felt there were additional valuables to be extracted. Most times, however, physical attack is a result of refusing to cooperate, or attempting resistance. In any event, the homeowner or resident would be unable to reach or use a weapon, and would be perhaps unsuccessful in any attempt to use one if the weapon was right at hand.

The record shows that while few criminal attacks in homes are prevented by the armed resistance of intended victims, use of personal weapons under agitated circumstances has resulted in innumerable incidents of accidental or mistaken shootings, with tragic effects. Many will recall the event some years ago in which a prominent and wealthy Long Island socialite, awakened by sounds in the house and fearful that a burglar had broken in, grabbed one of the family's hunting rifles for defense. Still dazed from sleep, and in a panic because of a recent rash of assaults in the neighborhood, she fired down a corridor as the sounds approached. The shot killed her husband, who had been up late, reading.

In the summer of 1970, a Washington, D.C. youth who was

very proud of the sports car he had been given as a present by his parents, heard sounds outside in the early morning and thought that someone was tampering with his precious car, which was parked in the driveway. The youth got his father's rifle and fired a shot through the window, which he later said was fired only as a "warning." The victim turned out to be a 14-year-old newsboy on his rounds delivering the morning papers.

The Weapon Quandary. Ownership of firearms is both a personal and community problem. For the individual, this many-sided question must be resolved generally by weighing the dangers that may be faced, the capability for controlled and effective defense if firearms are available, the responsibilities that are connected with possession of dangerous weapons including proper storage that makes the weapon instantly available when needed but always safe from unauthorized hands, especially from children.

Dr. Milton S. Eisenhower, chairman of the committee which made the study of violence, has stated in his report that no American should be allowed to own a handgun unless he can prove a need for it and meets stringent personal qualifications. He has endorsed proposals for uniform state laws making possession of a handgun illegal unless the owner is licensed by local police, and for confiscation of all guns not so licensed. This sensitive issue continues to plague the country, with little progress toward a satisfactory solution. The growth of crime, fostered in part by the availability of weapons, has prompted more law-abiding Americans to obtain arms for their own defense; thus the proliferation of weapons becomes a prime factor in both cause and effect of rampant crime.

Tear Gas and Mace. Frequent mentions of tear gas in news reports of riot control actions have prompted a widespread notion that the chemical makes a suitable personal defense weapon, that the gas incapacitates an attacker but is harmless to the user. But despite the extent of criminal assaults in the country, many communities have outlawed the use of tear gas by civilians, and made possession of such gas projectiles illegal.

These restrictions have a basis. Tear gas in the hands of an untrained person is not a dependable weapon, having a very limited range and unpredictable action; its use may result in effects that are contrary to those intended, often failing to halt a criminal while causing serious and permanent injury to the user or other innocent persons. What is worse is the tendency to use the weapon at any supposed provocation, often mistakenly.

Suppose you were to spray a container of the gas at a supposed attacker, and because of your inexperience or nervousness, fail to aim carefully so that the full effect of the shot is lost. Instead of incapacitating the attacker, this action may anger or provoke him to extreme physical action.

Pocket-size Gadget. For quite some time, mail order advertisements offered inexpensive tear gas projectors, small enough to be carried in a pocket or lady's handbag, and in handy pistol or fountain pen form. The wording and illustrations with these advertisements seemed to give assurance that firing off the contents of this projector would ward off any attack by disabling the criminal. Actually, the quantity of gas contained in the shell could not be depended upon to obtain the desired result.

A number of events led to a legal clampdown. More than one exceptionally fearful woman has let loose a spray of the gas in an elevator just because another occupant looked "suspicious." In the confined area of an elevator, the gas would affect the woman as much as the possible attacker. The tendency to hold the gas gun in her hand in tense and threatening situations made it too easy for thoughtless, impromptu action. It might be claimed that some assaults would have been prevented if the victim had such a weapon readily at hand, but it is possible also that many of these incidents might have been provoked by the mere move to "draw" such an undependable weapon.

Knives and Other Bladed Weapons. These meet the same objections as with tear gas, perhaps even more so. The use of a knife implies close-up, arm-to-arm encounter. Unless you can catch the intruder unawares, which is unlikely, and are very adept at using a knife or hatchet, you increase the jeopardy to yourself if you fail to fell him with a single stroke or blow. The weapon then may be seized and turned against you, or the assailant may himself be armed and will not hesitate to use a gun if he is cornered.

Your Legal Rights and Responsibilities. Defense of the home is your right in common law. You may wound or kill a burglar who breaks into your home, and not be subject to legal penalty. But there are many qualifications to these rights: Force may be used only to the extent needed to ward off an attack, or to permit escape from a definite danger of assault. A mere suspicion that a person is intending to attack is not sufficient to justify extreme measures. Suppose a neighbor coming home late at night and intoxicated goes to your home by mistake and tries to open a door with a key. Would you be justified in firing a shot through a window, wounding or killing him, under the impression that he was trying to break into your home? Suppose an apartment neighbor lost his key and was trying to get into his apartment down the fire escape, but mistook your window for his own and tried to force it open. Extreme actions, such as shooting, in those circumstances could be considered hasty and unwarranted, possibly involving you in criminal charges and perhaps also with a suit for civil damages.

Similarly, invasion of your grounds by children, even if they were to break into the basement on some lark or other, would not necessarily justify inflicting physical injury, since it might be held that you were not at any time in danger of an assault which was beyond your ability to repel by ordinary means.

The law is complicated and complex. You're not likely to start looking up law books, or call a lawyer, to find out what are your rights when danger threatens. No doubt you want to prevent physical injury to yourself and family, and protect your home. But you also need to avoid legal involvement for

injuring or killing anyone, even a burglar, if you can help it.
Then heed these basic cautions: make your house as safe as
possible from invasion. Avoid physical confrontation with
an intruder. Be cautious and restrained about resisting with
any weapon.